FROM JAZZ BABIES TO
GENERATION NEXT

FROM JAZZ BABIES TO
GENERATION NEXT

THE HISTORY OF THE
AMERICAN TEENAGER

LAURA B. EDGE

TWENTY-FIRST CENTURY BOOKS · MINNEAPOLIS

TO THE AWESOME TEENAGERS AT HOME RUN MINISTRIES, KINGWOOD, TEXAS

Twenty-First Century Books
A division of Lerner Publishing Group, Inc.
241 First Avenue North
Minneapolis, MN 55401 U.S.A.

Website address: www.lernerbooks.com

Library of Congress Cataloging-in-Publication Data

Edge, Laura Bufano, 1953–
    From jazz babies to generation next : the history of the American teenager / by Laura B. Edge.
        p.   cm. — (People's history)
    Includes bibliographical references and index.
    ISBN 978–0–7613–5868–8 (lib. bdg. : alk. paper)
    1. Teenagers—United States—Juvenile literature.
    2. Teenagers—United States—History—20th century.
    I. Title.
    HQ796.E284 2011
    305.2350973'0904—dc22   2010031144

Manufactured in the United States of America
1 – BP – 12/31/10

CONTENTS

*It was instilled in us that
work was necessary.
Everybody worked; it was a part of
life, for there was no life without it.*

—EDNA MATTHEWS CLIFTON, TEEN FROM RURAL TEXAS, 1883

GROWING UP FAST

Modern American teenagers are a driving force in the U.S. economy and culture. They spend billions of dollars each year on products and entertainment. Computers, video games, iPods, movies, music, skin and hair-care products, books, clothing, and cars are all designed to appeal to teens. And yet the word *teenager* is a recent invention. In the nineteenth century, young people between the ages of thirteen and nineteen were not called teenagers. The word did not exist. People were either children or adults.

In the past, childhood was considered to include the time up to eighteen, twenty-one, or even twenty-five years of age. A seventeen-year-old who lived at home and plowed the fields was considered an older boy. On the other hand, a fourteen-year-old who lived in a city and supported himself was called a young man.

The goal of childhood in the nineteenth century was to mold young people into good citizens. Good citizens were expected to contribute to society. Children took on adult responsibilities early. As soon as they were physically able, young people worked. They took jobs based on their physical size and strength rather than their age. For example, if strong enough, a young farmworker might operate dangerous equipment or work for hours in the field.

Children understood that their labor was essential to the survival of the family. Edna Matthews Clifton grew up on a Texas farm. She hand-washed dishes and clothes, mopped floors, made soap, and planted crops. She dreaded the hard labor of cotton harvest season. "Sometimes I would lie down on my sack [for gathering crops] and want to die," she said. "Sometimes they would pour water over my head to relieve me." But she picked cotton and corn for the sake of her family.

A Texas farm family poses in 1913 with the sacks they use to pick cotton. The youngest child, at age five, was expected to help. By the age of eleven, a child was expected to pick about 200 pounds (91 kilograms) of cotton per day.

A LITTLE SCHOOL, A LOT OF WORK

The majority of nineteenth-century children went to school between the ages of seven and fourteen. Few young people attended high school. Teens from wealthier families were more likely to stay in school. In 1890 just 6 percent of fourteen- to seventeen-year-olds attended high school in the United States. Only 3.5 percent graduated.

Many young people worked full-time outside of the home and contributed to the household income. Children generally entered the labor force sometime after the age of seven. They turned their wages over to their parents. "We were brought up in a large family," recalled Yvonne Dionne, a textile factory worker in New Hampshire. "As soon as one girl was old enough, she went to work. That was the way. The oldest one started, and the rest of the family had to follow suit. We didn't feel bad about not going to school because nobody could afford to. Our parents were too poor. None of us even finished grammar [grade] school."

In the late nineteenth century, economic hardships caused millions of Americans to leave their farms and head for cities to look for work. Eager to escape the racial discrimination and poverty of the South, African Americans flocked to northern cities. They were joined by millions of immigrants from southern and eastern Europe. The urban population of the United States increased dramatically. As a result, the U.S. economy shifted from a rural, agricultural base to an urban, manufacturing base.

Technological advances led to the growth of factories to produce goods. Machines took over work that was previously done by hand. Workers used power looms and sewing machines to make clothing. Factory workers also produced farm machinery, shoes, and cigars. In cities all across the United States, factory owners welcomed teen laborers. In many poor neighborhoods, practically every young person who had reached the age of fourteen worked in a factory. Most worked twelve hours a day, six days a week. "In such neighborhoods the joy of youth is well nigh extinguished," wrote social reformer Jane Addams, "and in that long procession of factory workers, each morning and evening, the young walk almost as wearily and listlessly as the old."

Immigrant teens became Americanized as quickly as possible. They learned English and adjusted to the culture of the United States faster than their parents did. They wore American clothes, read American books and newspapers, and adopted an American spirit of independence. Many teens saw their parents as old fashioned. Generational conflicts arose because the older generation wanted to preserve their old-country values and traditions. "Now that you have become Americanized," an Italian mother told her son, "you understand everything and I understand nothing." For some African Americans, the older generation was made up of former slaves who had grown up on plantations. The children were free-born urban Americans. Conflicts were inevitable.

Beginning in the 1880s, many Native American youth were sent to boarding schools, such as the Carlisle Indian Industrial School in Pennsylvania *(above)*, run by the U.S. government. Separated from their families, the children were forced to speak English instead of their own language and to act and dress like white Americans. The schools also trained students for low-income jobs.

FUN AND GAMES

Many nineteenth-century teens spent most of their time working, but they still found time for fun. Reading was a popular leisure activity. Dime novels—books that sold for ten cents—hooked readers with patriotic themes and tales of adventure. Boys read stories about Buffalo Bill Cody and the taming of the Wild West. Horatio Alger books were also popular. His stories feature poor boys who overcome adversity and find success.

Boys also played sports. Baseball was the national favorite. Teens organized their own games with little or no adult supervision. In some cities, the Young Men's Christian Association (YMCA) provided athletic programs for boys between the ages of ten and sixteen. Churches and settlement houses (community centers) also formed clubs for working-class boys. The Boys' Club at Hull House in Chicago, Illinois, for example, had clubrooms, game rooms, a billiard room, a bowling alley, a band room, a library, a woodshop, and a printing shop. Teens hung out together and played pool or table tennis. They played basketball, learned to play a musical instrument, and read books or newspapers.

Nineteenth-century boys enjoyed more freedom and independence than girls of the era. Teen girls could only socialize under the watchful supervision of adults. Walking, ice-skating, roller-skating, tennis, and croquet were considered appropriate exercise for girls because the activities were not too strenuous. Bicycling

Baseball was a popular sport across the United States in the nineteenth century. These young men played for Morris Brown College in Atlanta, Georgia.

became hugely popular at the end of the nineteenth century. Parents worried about this newfangled invention, however. They feared for their daughters' purity when they exposed their ankles and legs while riding bicycles.

Lucy Larcom was one of many girls unhappy with the restrictions placed on her life at puberty. "I clung to the child's inalienable privilege of running half wild; and when I found that I really was growing up, I felt quite rebellious. I was as tall as a woman at thirteen, and my older sisters insisted upon lengthening my dresses, and putting up my mop of hair with a comb. I felt injured and almost outraged."

These nineteenth-century girls are doing activities that were considered appropriate for young ladies at the time—needlework and letter writing.

YOUNG VAGABONDS

For poor city youth, survival took precedence over fun. In the late nineteenth century, many young people lived with their families in crowded city slums. They learned to fend for themselves. Extreme poverty forced many adolescents to roam the streets. Some supported themselves by selling newspapers, polishing boots, or doing errands. Others joined gangs and became thieves and criminals. Charles Loring Brace, a writer, humanitarian, and philanthropist, claimed that the "dangerous classes of

After witnessing New York City gang violence firsthand, a newspaper artist illustrated it for *Frank Leslie's Illustrated Newspaper* in the 1850s.

New York" were its young people between the ages of eight and seventeen. New York City's newspapers and magazines called these street kids "young vagabonds."

Brace warned that if society did not feed, clothe, and educate young street boys, they would become a serious threat when they matured. "They will poison society," he wrote. "They will perhaps be embittered at the wealth and the luxuries they never share. Then let society beware, when the outcast, vicious, reckless multitude of New York boys, swarming now in every foul alley and low street, come to know their power *and use it!*"

Brace, Jane Addams, and other urban reformers were also concerned about the problem of crime for adolescent girls. In large cities, some older women trained girls between the ages of twelve and seventeen to be pickpockets—to steal money and watches from people's pockets on the streets. Girls also learned how to steal handkerchiefs, furs, and purses. They lifted merchandise from the counters of department stores.

Some poor young women also slipped into casual prostitution as a way to earn money for necessities, luxuries, or amusements. In a practice called treating, the women exchanged sexual favors with men for dinner, clothing, or a night on the town. Reformers looked for ways to save these "wayward girls" from ruin.

Photojournalist Jacob Riis took photographs of inner-city youth and published them in the 1890 book *How the Other Half Lives.* His gritty photos opened America's eyes to an entire youth subculture. Riis was convinced that the poor living conditions in urban slums affected young people in negative ways and led to violence, crime, and alcohol abuse.

The "problem of youth" became a much discussed topic all across the United States. Middle-class parents

Jane Addams *(left)* talks to children at Hull House. Addams and Ellen Gates Starr founded Hull House on the West Side of Chicago, Illinois, in 1889. Addams and Starr were social reformers interested in the rights of children and in public health. Hull House volunteers taught classes to lower-income residents, hosted clubs and cultural programs, and conducted studies on social issues.

feared juvenile delinquency was contagious. They worried that the bad habits of poor urban youth might catch on with their children. This led to a child-saving movement—a massive effort by psychologists, urban reformers, and educators to save urban working-class youth from the moral and physical dangers of city life. "Every city is full of young people who are utterly bewildered and uninstructed," wrote Jane Addams. "We may either smother the divine fire of youth or we may feed it."

CHAPTER
TWO

Our elders are always optimistic in their views of the present, pessimistic in their views of the future; youth is pessimistic toward the present and gloriously hopeful for the future.

—WRITER RANDOLPH S. BOURNE, BLOOMFIELD, NEW JERSEY, 1913

THE AGE OF ADOLESCENCE

As part of their effort to save at-risk urban youth, reformers studied the high crime rate among young people. "Much of it," wrote educator Irving King, "is not the expression of a really vicious nature, but of the misguided impulse to find adventure, to see life, to do something big and startling."

Until the late nineteenth century, teens who committed crimes were sent to adult jails and prisons. Reformers realized that locking up young offenders in adult prisons was a bad idea. Teens learned from older inmates, and many left prison as more hardened and skillful criminals. Jane Addams, Julia Lathrop, and a group of women from Hull House pressured Illinois legislators to create a separate court for young people under the age of sixteen. In 1899 the Juvenile Court Act established the first juvenile court in the United States. The law stated that "no child under sixteen years of age should be considered or treated as a criminal; that, under that age, he should not be arrested, indicted [charged], convicted, imprisoned, or punished as one."

The Juvenile Court Act helped foster the idea that the teen years were a separate stage of life. Psychologists, social workers, and educators began to study thirteen- to nineteen-year-olds as a separate and distinct group. Teens, they discovered, shared common characteristics and had unique problems and needs.

A NEW BIRTH

In 1904 psychologist G. Stanley Hall, president of Clark University in Massachusetts, published the book *Adolescence*. In it, he defined adolescence as the years between fourteen and twenty-four. Hall called adolescence, "a marvelous new birth." But he also described it as "the age of sentiment and of religion, of rapid fluctuation of mood. . . . Youth awakes to a new world and understands neither it nor himself."

Hall popularized the view that adolescence was a time of crisis. For proof, he gathered statistics on the increase of illegal acts committed by twelve- to fourteen-year-olds. Hall called the teen years "a stormy period of great agitation, when the very worst and best impulses in the human soul struggle against each other for its possession."

Hall feared that poor urban teens were forced to grow up too quickly. Snatched out of childhood by the need to work full-time, young people were not able to enjoy the benefits of a complete childhood. He favored a protected adolescence and a gradual rise to adulthood. Hall wanted teens out of factories and into schools.

A SHIFT IN LABOR

In the early twentieth century, attitudes about child labor began to change. Photojournalist Lewis Hine documented child workers through

A teenage girl works in a mill in South Carolina in 1908. Lewis Hine took this and many other photographs to bring attention to the dangers child laborers faced in the early 1900s.

a series of compelling photographs. His stark images of grimy children, looking tiny and helpless beside huge industrial machines, shed light on the problem of child labor. In 1904 the National Child Labor Committee mounted an anti-child-labor movement. Reformers lobbied (pushed) for laws that would raise the age at which children could work full-time.

Social reformers Florence Kelley and Alzina Stevens studied wage-earning children in Chicago. They wrote about the children they saw working long hours in unsafe conditions. Their reports led to change. The U.S. Congress passed the Keating-Owen Act in 1916. This federal child labor law set the minimum working age at fourteen for factories and sixteen for mines. Some factory owners ignored the law and hired underage workers, but the number of ten- to thirteen-year-old workers decreased.

Older teens filled the gap in the workplace. A large number of factories employed both men and women, and the workplace became a social outlet for teens. Young people sat together on lunch breaks and chatted about novels, films, and music. Girls showed off new hats and shoes. They shared shopping tips, tidbits of news, and exchanged personal stories.

THE GROWTH OF HIGH SCHOOLS

Reformers also worked to make school attendance mandatory up to the age of sixteen. State lawmakers passed school attendance laws to keep young people in school. As a result, high school enrollment increased. By 1910, 14 percent of the teen population attended high school. Although the number of young people in school more than doubled, the dropout rate remained high. In some cities, 88 percent of high school students did not graduate.

In the early twentieth century, educators disagreed about the goal of high school. Some argued that it should prepare students for adult life. Others felt it should prepare them for college. The majority of schools adopted a traditional, classical curriculum that included the study of Latin (the ancient language then commonly used in higher education and the sciences). Students could also choose electives—classes not required by the curriculum. As a result of these curriculum standards, high school students all across the United States shared a fairly similar course of study.

In addition to academic study, high schools offered a variety of activities for students to explore. Competitive sports, student government, debate teams, drama clubs, and school newspapers all appeared in high schools. These groups allowed students to try different skills and find their strengths.

FASHION AND ADVERTISING

In previous generations, teens had worn clothing that they or their mothers had sewn at home. In the early 1900s, U.S. manufacturers began to produce inexpensive, ready-made clothing. Common styles of ready-to-wear clothes developed. Many young women dressed like the fictional Gibson girl featured in popular magazine illustrations. The Gibson girl wore a long, elegant dress tightly cinched at the waist. Her glossy hair

Artist Charles Dana Gibson (1867–1944) created the Gibson girl as a magazine illustration. Many Gibson girl illustrations, such as the one above, appeared in magazines in the early 1900s. Many young American women considered the Gibson girl an ideal—beautiful and stylish, with an air of independence.

was piled in loose curls atop her head. She was refined and stylish, and many American girls wanted to look like her.

Under their clothes, young women wore corsets. Corsets are tube-shaped undergarments that, at the time, were made of heavy cotton twill. The fabric was reinforced with bands of steel or whalebone. Corsets of this period were designed to mold a woman's body into an S-shape: an ample bust, flat stomach, tiny waist, and rounded rear. Corsets were heavy, hot, and uncomfortable. Sometimes they were laced so tightly that they broke the wearer's ribs. Over time, tight corsets could also damage a woman's internal organs.

Young people used fashion to create an image. For young women, it was an era of curls, frills, ribbons, heeled boots, enormous hats, ornamental purses, bangles, and very long gloves. According to Jane Addams, "Through the huge hat, with its wilderness of bedraggled feathers, the girl announces to the world that she is here. She demands attention to the fact of her existence, she states that she is ready to live, to take her place in the world." Young men wore jackets, knee pants or trousers, and flat caps or bowler hats—often in black, gray, or brown. But a dandy could spruce up his traditional male clothing with colored waistcoats (vests), scarves, and jewelry.

For many parents, clothing was a necessity, not a fashion statement. Working teens who used a portion of their wages on clothing and entertainment clashed with their parents over spending. The young often felt that they worked long hours to earn their wages and deserved to spend a portion of it as they wished. Many parents, on the other hand, expected their children to turn over all their wages to the family.

Whatever parents thought of their children's spending, advertisers saw the potential of young shoppers. The advertising industry expanded to include teen spenders. New ads went beyond simply delivering information. They sought to influence adolescent behavior. Ads sent the message that access to certain products and services would transform everyday life. By using their own money, teens could decide how they looked and how they socialized. Teens began to link independence with spending.

THE NICKEL SHOW

Urban young people in the early 1900s did not make a lot of money, but they spent what they could on fun. Technological advances gave them many new leisure activities to enjoy. Teens went to movie theaters, dance halls, penny arcades, ice cream parlors, and amusements parks.

Teens flocked to nickelodeons, motion picture theaters where moviegoers could watch films for a nickel. In the early 1900s, business owners began opening movie houses all across the United States and the theater became the social center of many neighborhoods. Films of this era were silent and ran between ten and twelve minutes. A popular series of films, *The Perils of Pauline*, thrilled audiences with a new adventure every other week. Pauline, a young, excitement-loving heiress, was tied to train tracks in one episode and nearly cut to pieces by a buzz saw in another. She was blown up at sea by mad pirates, thrown off a cliff, and trapped in a runaway hot-air balloon. In every episode, her handsome stepbrother and suitor, Harry, saved her in the nick of time. The films were simple and predictable, but teen audiences loved them.

Shows ran continuously from morning until evening. The theater provided young people with beauty, adventure, and romance. Viewers were transported, temporarily, to another world and could escape the drudgery of long days of work. According to Jane Addams, "The theater becomes to them a 'veritable [real] house of dreams' infinitely more real than the noisy streets and the crowded factories."

Groups of young people attended the same theater night after night. They identified with the grainy characters on the screen who taught them how to think, act, and feel. This shared leisure experience bound young people as a group. Teens began to identify with one another rather than with adults.

Many adults observed youth's quest for fun with concern. They saw fun as a path that led straight to disaster. Since hard work was prized as a virtue, time wasted lounging in a nickelodeon was considered pure laziness by some. It could only lead to a life of idleness. The Juvenile Protection Agency recommended that young people under the age of nineteen not be allowed to enter a nickelodeon without an adult chaperone.

MUSIC AND DANCING

Movies were not the only popular teen amusement. In the early twentieth century, ragtime music exploded as a national craze. The syncopated (varying or irregular) rhythm of the music appealed to teens, and the music industry expanded rapidly. Popular songs became a part of the nation's shared culture.

With ragtime music came the so-called animal dances: the turkey trot, the bunny hug, the grizzly bear, and the monkey glide. Dance halls sprouted up where teens could hang out together, listen to music, and dance without adult supervision. The halls gave teens a place where they could socialize with people their age. It was also a way for young men and women to meet.

Many adults objected to ragtime music, dance halls, and animal dances. The music was not considered respectable for teens. According to the magazine the *Musical Courier*, "A wave of vulgar, filthy and suggestive music has inundated [taken over] the land." Members of the American Federation of Musicians were encouraged to

Scott Joplin (1867-1917) was known as the King of Ragtime. Joplin's sophisticated musical pieces were widely popular and helped shape ragtime in the early 1900s. His *Maple Leaf Rag*, first published in 1899, sold steadily for more than thirty years.

"make every effort to suppress and to discourage the playing and the publishing of such musical trash."

Parents and reformers feared that dance halls were a bad influence on young people and would lead to a breakdown in morality. They found the dances sexually suggestive. While dancing, young men and young women embraced. They wiggled, hopped, strutted, and shook. Adults worried that ragtime promoted sex and wild behavior. Some feared their daughters would fall into prostitution.

Groups of adults mounted campaigns to ban several popular dances. In Philadelphia, Pennsylvania, newspapers reported that "the turkey trot and the grizzly bear will no longer be tolerated in society here." In New York, the Committee of Amusements tried to replace "freakish and degrading dances" with respectable ballroom dances such as the waltz and the fox-trot. They rented ballrooms "to illustrate the other side, the beautiful and decent as against the ugly and degraded." Reformers also worked to close dance halls and replace them with respectable dance socials held in settlement houses and schools. Chaperoned by adults, these dances would provide a safe, wholesome outlet for the adolescent need for fun.

Some adults objected to ragtime music and dance halls simply because they drew young people away from the home. Dance halls were not multigenerational. They were filled with young people. Most of the teens who went to dance halls lived in crowded slums. They had no privacy at home and no way to create an identity of their own, separate from the family unit. Dance halls filled their need for a bit of separation from their parents. But many of the parents felt that their teen children still belonged at home.

In spite of adult objections, teens flocked to dance halls. They enjoyed the fun, the freedom, and the chance to socialize with other young people. Teens were beginning to form their own distinct culture, separate and apart from both childhood and adulthood.

Everybody wants to be young, now—though they want all us young people to be something else. Funny, isn't it?

—YOUNG FLAPPER JANE, FROM THE EAST COAST, 1925

CHAPTER
THREE

THE JAZZ AGE

In 1914 war broke out in Europe. Most of the world's great powers were drawn into the conflict, which came to be called the Great War (and later, World War I). The Great War pitted the Allies (the United Kingdom, France, Russia, the United States, and others) against the Central powers (Germany, the Austro-Hungarian Empire, the Ottoman Empire, and others). By the time the Allies won the war in 1918, more than 15 million people were dead.

U.S. soldiers returned home. The hardships and sacrifices their families made during the war were over. The U.S. economy began to grow, and Americans began spending freely. Some people, such as white farmers and African Americans, still struggled economically. But many Americans entered the 1920s—the Roaring Twenties—almost giddy with optimism.

Technological advances led to all kinds of new products to make life easier and more enjoyable. It was the era of the automobile and the airplane. Families traveled and took vacations together. Washing machines, home refrigerators, and vacuum cleaners eased the burden of household chores. Young people had more time to simply enjoy life.

Everyone wanted to be "modern" and own the latest high-tech products. Those who could not afford to pay for them bought on credit. They paid a small amount to take the item home and then made monthly payments for the balance. "America was going on the greatest, gaudiest spree in history," wrote novelist F. Scott Fitzgerald.

WHERE'S THE PARTY?

Teens loved Fitzgerald's novels, and his books personified the decade. His characters drank, smoked, drove fast cars, listened to jazz music, and danced until dawn. All this partying took place during Prohibition, which went into effect in 1920. This new U.S. law made it illegal to make, transport, or sell alcoholic beverages.

This advertisement for Paige automobiles appeared in the *Ladies Home Journal* in 1927. Middle-class Americans spent freely during the Roaring Twenties on new and improved technology such as cars and washing machines.

In spite of Prohibition, Americans drank more than ever. Organized crime controlled a multimillion-dollar illegal business. They produced bootleg (illegally made) liquor and smuggled it from state to state. Speakeasies, or illegal bars, sprang up all over the country. Some people made their own liquor and drank at home.

Adolescents found the mixed messages of Prohibition hypocritical. The law told Americans not to drink, and yet young people saw flasks of illegal liquor everywhere. And people drank to get drunk, an experience that became commonplace. Following adult examples, some teens snuck alcohol from their parents and drank in secret.

Teens also wanted to enjoy the social freedoms of the Roaring Twenties. Automobiles became more common, and young people borrowed their parents' cars. Cars gave young people a private place to meet their friends and sweethearts. They could enjoy themselves without adult supervision. A new system of dating developed. Teens went out with one another without chaperones, and premarital sex increased. Teens experimented with sex at lovers' lanes (remote outdoor areas) and at petting parties (gatherings where couples kissed and fondled).

As a further mark of their growing subculture, young people developed their own slang. For example, if something was extraordinary or wonderful, it was "the bee's knees," the "berries," or "the cat's meow." Someone who was nervous had the "heebie-jeebies," and a person who looked elegant or fashionable was "spiffy." A person with "it" had sex appeal.

These young women were photographed in Harlem, a New York City neighborhood, in the late 1920s. They wear the flapper "uniform"—tightly fitted cloche hats, wrapover coats, and strapped shoes.

FLAPPERS

The 1920s saw a dramatic change in young women's dress and appearance. Gone were tight corsets and floor-length dresses.

College-age women wore thin, short, sleeveless dresses that showed off their necks, arms, backs, and calves. They added silk stockings held up by garters, high-heeled shoes, strings of long beads, and bangle bracelets. Wide hat brims disappeared. Young women cut their hair in short bobs and wore small, close-fitting hats called cloches. The press dubbed these young women flappers. Flappers who liked music and dancing were called jazz babies.

High school girls admired the flapper style. But there were no teen stores with clothing designed for their changing bodies. They had to choose between large sizes in children's clothing or small sizes in women's. Teens fought with their parents over appropriate clothing. The new fashions reflected a changing morality, and many parents found them brazen and immodest. "Girls have more nerve nowadays—look at their clothes!" said one mother. Another mother agreed. "We can't keep our boys decent when girls dress that way."

All across the country, civic leaders passed decency codes to regulate immodest styles. At public beaches, park officials measured girls' bathing suits to make sure hemlines were not too many inches above the girls' knees. If a bathing suit failed the test, the girl was arrested for indecent exposure. Lawmakers in Utah introduced a bill that called for fines and imprisonment for any young woman who went out in public wearing "skirts higher than three inches [8 centimeters] above the ankle." In Virginia, regulations specified how much of a girl's throat could be exposed.

Lipstick and rouge, once only worn by prostitutes and actresses, became the vogue. Magazines

A police officer in West Palm Beach, Florida, measures the distance from a young woman's bathing suit to her knees in this 1925 photo. Decency laws throughout the United States limited how women could dress.

and newspapers filled with ads for products that promised to make average girls look "modern." Stores sold face cream, lipstick, perfume, and eyeliner. Cosmetics became acceptable for teens.

Many adolescents in the 1920s smoked cigarettes. Cigarettes became a symbol of masculinity for young men and of liberation for teen girls. Advertisements portrayed cigarettes as a fashion accessory for the modern woman. Young girls wanted the slim, boyish figure of the flapper, so advertisers played up to that desire. Cigarette manufacturer Lucky Strike encouraged women to "Reach for a Lucky Instead of a Sweet!"

Babe Ruth, shown here in 1927, played for the New York Yankees for most of his career. Baseball's popularity, the Yankees' success, and Ruth's larger-than-life personality made him one of the top U.S. sports heroes of the 1920s.

LISTENING FUN

Flappers and their male admirers were able to enjoy a new form of entertainment. On November 2, 1920, station KDKA in Pittsburgh, Pennsylvania, ushered in the age of radio. The station first broadcast the election results for the U.S. presidential race between Warren G. Harding and James M. Cox. Entertainment programs soon followed. By the end of the decade, radio stations were broadcasting news, music, sports, and comedy and drama shows from coast to coast.

Radio changed the way young people got news. Teens no longer had to read the newspaper to learn about Charles Lindbergh's successful solo airplane flight from New York to Paris, France. They listened to the radio instead. Teens listened to baseball games or tapped their feet to the beat of a new song. Radio brought the world into their living rooms.

But young people didn't spend all their time listening to the radio. They also flocked to sporting events. Baseball was king, and Babe Ruth was the king of baseball. In 1927 Ruth slammed sixty home runs and set a record that stood for more than thirty years. Teen boys followed his career and kept up with his statistics. Young people also spent their free time working crossword puzzles, playing with yo-yos, and roller-skating. And marathon contests became a craze. Contestants competed to see who could kiss the longest, dance for days without stopping, or sit on a flagpole for extended lengths of time.

MOVIES

Movies emerged as the country's most popular form of entertainment in the 1920s. Films were black and white, as color technology hadn't yet been developed. Early in the decade, movies were also silent—meaning they had no sound track that included actors' voices, music, or sound effects. Instead, filmmakers inserted printed captions between scenes to help tell the story. Theaters also hired musicians, live actors speaking dialogue, and sound effects specialists to make the movies more exciting.

Swashbucklers (adventure films featuring sword fights), historical extravaganzas, comedies, romances, and mysteries were popular with moviegoers. Many films also showed a lot of drinking, dancing, and partying. One movie billboard advertised "brilliant men, beautiful jazz babies, champagne baths, midnight revels, petting parties in the purple dawn, all ending in one terrific smashing climax that makes you gasp."

Many teens went to the movies several times a week. They watched how their favorite stars danced, drank, kissed, and flirted. It was the beginning of the celebrity culture. Adolescents read about movie stars in magazines and copied their clothing and mannerisms. Styles that appeared in films quickly became the latest fad.

Clara Bow and Rudolph Valentino were the first movie stars to be marketed for their sex appeal. She was the It Girl, and the

Actress Clara Bow is shown here in the late 1930s. As the It Girl, Bow symbolized the self-confident and sexually attractive young woman.

In this 1926 photo, three young women cry over the death of movie star Rudolph Valentino. Known as the Latin Lover because of his dark good looks, Valentino was famous for playing romantic, passionate characters. His death at age thirty-one sent his female fans into mourning.

Italian Valentino was the Latin Lover. When Valentino died unexpectedly in 1926, an estimated 100,000 people filed past his coffin. That number included a huge crowd of adolescent girls. They filled the streets outside the funeral home to view his body. Some became hysterical, and the scene turned chaotic.

In 1927 Warner Brothers released *The Jazz Singer*, starring Al Jolson. It was the world's first feature-length talkie, or film with a sound track. Jolson spoke the first words ever heard in a film: "Wait a minute! Wait a minute! You ain't heard nothin' yet." By the end of the decade, silent films had disappeared and sound movies were firmly entrenched as an important part of youth culture.

MUSIC AND DANCING

Music was everywhere in the 1920s, and jazz was the music of choice. Looser and wilder than ragtime, jazz quickly became popular with young people. Jazz musicians traveled from the African American community of New Orleans, Louisiana, to Chicago, New York, and other northern cities. They opened jazz clubs and thrilled listeners with syncopated rhythms and wailing saxophones.

Many parents objected to jazz music. They worried that it corrupted their children. An article in the *Ladies' Home Journal* claimed that "never in the history of our land have there been such immoral conditions among our young people, and in the surveys made by many organizations regarding these conditions, the blame is laid on jazz music and its evil influence on the young people of to-day." Their parents' objections only increased teens' infatuation with jazz.

Dancing was a key part of a young person's social life in the 1920s. With the new shorter skirts, girls showed off their legs in the kicky, high-stepping moves of the Charleston. In another popular dance, the Black Bottom, dancers stomped their feet and swiveled their hips. They danced close together, body to body, cheek to cheek. Many parents criticized the dances. According to the *Catholic Telegraph* of Cincinnati, Ohio, "The music is sensuous, the embracing of partners—the female only half dressed—is absolutely indecent; and the motions—they are such as may not be described, with any respect for propriety [decency], in a family newspaper."

Young girls do the Charleston on the street in Harlem, New York, in the 1920s. The Charleston and other dances of the 1920s were popular with American teens because they allowed more freedom of movement. Many parents thought the dances were immoral, however.

Young people argued with their parents over dancing. Teens did not believe it corrupted them. They danced to have fun. According to a sixteen-year-old girl from Denver, Colorado, "*Most* of us girls don't get any special thrill out of close dancing. We do get a thrill out of the dancing itself; and we go to parties with these young crumpet munchers and snuggle pups [slang terms for young men] because we like to dance, and for no other reason."

A CLASH OF CULTURES

High school enrollment continued to rise at a steady pace in the 1920s. By the end of the decade, approximately half of the teen population attended high school. Home and family became less important to adolescents than their friends. Teens were economically dependent on their parents. But they were not as willing as previous generations to submit to their authority. Movies, dances, and cars all drew young people away from the home. As one high school girl complained to her mother, "What on earth *do* you want me to do? Just sit around home all evening!"

Some adolescents questioned adult authority and challenged the strict rules of the older generation. Teens felt they had the right to make their own decisions and their own mistakes. "Please try to realize," wrote a group of teens in *Parents* magazine, "that apart from the necking, jazz-mad, superficial, date-crazy, gum-chewing part of us there is another side which is essentially fine and sincere. . . . We have to explore and discover for ourselves what is good."

Many adults feared that the moral fiber of the country was in danger. They worried about the growing independence of young women. Women were considered morally superior to men, and many people looked to women to uphold the nation's standards of decency. Adults feared that if adolescent girls abandoned the values of their parents, then the social order of the country would surely crumble.

In 1924 a startling event brought the focus of the nation onto America's youth. Bobby Franks, a fourteen-year-old boy from Chicago, Illinois, was found murdered. Police traced evidence back to two of Bobby's neighbors—nineteen-year-old Nathan Leopold and eighteen-year-old Richard Loeb. Leopold and Loeb were from wealthy families, and both were students at the prestigious University of Chicago. After their arrests, the young men confessed to kidnapping and killing Bobby. They said that the murder was part of a detailed plot. The pair had thought up this "perfect crime" just to prove that they could get away with it. But their

Richard Loeb *(left)* and Nathan Leopold *(right)* murdered a young neighbor in May 1924. Both teenagers were extremely intelligent, and Loeb was fascinated by crime stories. Both admitted that they had no real motive for the murder—that it was almost a game to plan and carry out the crime.

plot failed, and Leopold and Loeb were sentenced to life in prison.

The case generated a tremendous amount of press coverage and sparked a fierce debate about the younger generation. Judge Ben Lindsey saw the case as a wake-up call for the nation. "It is a new kind of murder with a new kind of cause," he wrote. "That cause is to be found in the modern mentality and modern freedom of youth."

For many people, the Bobby Franks murder was the result of the excitement-seeking, party-crazy, dance-mad youth culture of the Roaring Twenties. In October 1929, those free and easy days came to a screeching halt. The stock market crashed, and panic hit the banking and finance industries. The economy began to crumble. In the coming years, adolescents would face a host of challenges they never dreamed of.

We are way far back in rent. . . .
Every week we go to bed one
or two days without anything to eat.
My brother and I go down
to the railroad track
to pick up coal to keep warm.

—A.M., AN EIGHTH-GRADE STUDENT FROM COLORADO, IN A
LETTER TO ELEANOR ROOSEVELT (WIFE OF U.S. PRESIDENT
FRANKLIN D. ROOSEVELT), 1935

CHAPTER
FOUR

SURVIVING HARD TIMES

The 1930s was a time of anxiety for teens and for most other Americans. The stock market crash set in motion a long-term economic decline called the Great Depression (1929–1942). During the Depression, banks closed and businesses failed. Thousands of Americans lost their jobs. By 1933 between 25 and 33 percent of Americans were out of work. In some cities, the unemployment rate reached 50 percent. Families faced losing their homes. Many could barely find enough food to eat. In rural areas, some teens ate weeds or hunted rabbits and squirrels. In cities they sifted through garbage cans or stood in relief lines, hoping for a bowl of soup or a piece of bread.

People on the lowest rung of the employment ladder—women, African Americans, and teens—had the hardest time finding employment. President Franklin D. Roosevelt's New Deal economic programs focused on providing jobs for married men with families. As a result, teens found it nearly impossible to find work. Hundreds, sometimes even thousands, of young people lined up each day in front of potential workplaces looking for jobs.

As more and more people struggled financially, families moved into smaller homes or apartments. Some lost their homes and were forced to live in small, makeshift dwellings called shanties. Shanties were built from packing crates, flattened tin cans, and tar paper. Groups of shanties—known as shantytowns—sprang up on unused lands, usually within cities. In close quarters and with less privacy, teens and their parents argued more. "I'd give anything if I had a job," said a girl from Chicago. "I wouldn't live here, you bet, with ma complaining all the time because there ain't enough money, and pa sore [angry] because we always have the same old potatoes and gravy and bread pudding for dinner."

Hungry people line up for free food in New York City in the early 1930s. With families facing high unemployment during the Depression, teens struggled with food shortages, homelessness, and other hardships.

ON THE ROAD

During the 1930s, an estimated 250,000 young people left home and wandered the country looking for work. Most of them were adolescent boys, but girls fled too, often dressed in boys' clothes. They represented a small percentage of the total teen population, but these young drifters were a highly visible minority. Adults worried about the effects these "wild children of America" would have on their communities.

This 1937 photograph shows a family traveling through New Mexico to find work in cotton fields. Many American families left home to find work in other parts of the country during the Depression.

Teen wanderers hitchhiked or hopped freight trains to get from one town to the next. "The quickest and easiest way to get out was to jump a train and go somewhere," recalled sixteen-year-old Jim Mitchell. "We thought it was the magic carpet—the click of the rails—romance." They slept in parks, alleys, and boxcars. Thousands died from illnesses or accidents.

The biggest problem they faced was finding food and shelter. "I was hungry all the time," said John Fawcett, a drifter from West Virginia. "Dreadfully hungry. I'd never been hungry before. I went two or three days without anything to eat. In a short time on the road, I lost fifteen to twenty pounds [7 to 9 kg]." Young drifters also had to dodge the law. Townspeople resented the daily flow of hungry visitors. Police officers arrested many transients, tossed them into local jails, or forced them out of town.

To find food, some young people followed the harvesting season and picked fruit or vegetables in California, Texas, and other states with warm climates. Others did odd jobs for a meal or two. They ate at soup kitchens and missions (community centers run by churches or religious groups). They also snatched apples as they tramped through the fields. Some, desperate for food and shelter, begged or stole to survive. "It ain't stealing when you're hungry and willing to work and you can't get nothing to eat," said a drifter named Tony. "You don't take nothing away from anybody who needs it. You just ask enough to live on. That's all. And you are willing to work; if you can't get work, why, you're entitled to help yourself."

STAY IN SCHOOL!

Many young people in the 1930s admitted they felt discouraged and bitter. Concerned adults turned to the government for help. In 1935 Roosevelt launched the National Youth Administration (NYA) to keep at-risk teens in school. Under the plan, high school students whose families were in financial need worked in clerical or student service jobs for six dollars a month. They washed windows, delivered messages, graded papers, or acted as nurse's aides. The money they earned helped them purchase food, clothing, shoes, and books. It was often the only thing that kept them in school. According to an eleventh-grade student from Iowa, "When I started school in September, I did not know whether I was going to continue to go or not. When I got my first [NYA] check I was so tickled I could have shouted. I went to town that very evening and got some bread for my brothers' and sisters' and my own lunches."

In the days before email, Twitter, and texting, a teen waits to deliver a telegram in the 1930s. Many young people found jobs under Roosevelt's National Youth Administration plan.

Many teens copied the styles of movie stars, such as film star Anita Page *(above)*. Page's belted calf-length dress was a very fashionable style in the 1930s.

By 1936, 65 percent of fourteen- to seventeen-year-olds attended high school (although the figure was much lower for African American teens in the rural South). For the first time in history, the majority of teens spent a large portion of their day with people their own age. They looked to one another for advice and approval. Continuing the trend that drew teens closer to one another and farther away from their parents, many young people adopted the values of their peers.

FADS AND FUN

Despite economic hardships, teens still followed fads and fashions. And teens from middle- and upper-class families not that hard-hit by the Depression still spent money. Department stores experimented with high school clothing shops to reach teen buyers. Stocked with styles and sizes designed to appeal to adolescents, these retail spaces were the first to specifically target teens.

Teens saw fashion as a tool they could use to create an image, and owning the right clothes became important to high schoolers. They faced peer pressure to be popular and dress alike. For girls this meant calf-length belted dresses or skirts with blouses or sweaters. To complete the ensemble, girls wore ankle socks and saddle shoes. High school boys wore wide-legged, high-waisted pants. Those who could afford it added sweater vests.

High schools also provided teens a place where they could talk about their interests, share their hobbies, and create fads. One new pastime was the board game Monopoly. The game was designed in 1933 by Charles B. Darrow, an unemployed salesman, and manufactured by Parker Brothers. Monopoly was based on the idea of buying and selling real estate. Young people liked the idea of a game where they could pretend to make a fortune with a few rolls of the dice. The game became so popular that stores couldn't keep it on the shelves. Teens also played miniature golf, worked jigsaw puzzles, and tried their luck at pinball machines.

Superman and Batman debuted as comic-book characters in the 1930s. The superheroes were instant hits with teens, and comic-book sales exploded. Paperback books were also popular. They fit in a coat pocket and sold for twenty-five cents in drugstores, department stores, and newsstands. Teenagers read many mysteries in the 1930s. Girls could not get enough of Nancy Drew, a feisty sixteen-year-old detective who was smart, resourceful, and independent. Adolescent boys followed the fictional exploits of the Hardy Boys. Frank and Joe Hardy, brothers and amateur detectives, kept teens turning the pages of one adventure after another.

A group of boys play miniature golf on a homemade course in Ohio in the 1930s. During the Depression, children and teens found cheap ways to have fun—such as flying kites, roller- and ice-skating, and playing board games.

MOVIES

Young people did not have a lot of money to spend on entertainment. But they scrimped and saved to have fun. During the Depression, movies were the most popular form of entertainment. Young people went to the movies to help them escape the realities of a hard life. Teens who could afford it went often, the majority at least once a week. For twenty cents, they could watch two feature films, a newsreel, a cartoon, a short film, and coming attractions—and still have money for candy.

Movies reached a new level of sophistication in the 1930s. They had compelling story lines, lavish sets, original music, and stunning special effects. Dracula, King Kong, and Frankenstein all made their movie debuts in the 1930s. The Marx Brothers—real-life brothers who acted under the names Groucho, Chico, Harpo, and Zeppo—starred in a string of slapstick comedies. Teens loved the brothers' wise-cracking putdowns and antic physical comedy. Gangster films especially appealed to city youth. In these films, adolescent boys drift into crime because of the influence of adult criminals. Crime was seen as alluring and acceptable, despite the danger.

In contrast to the "bad" kids depicted in gangster films, teens also enjoyed watching "good" kids in movies. Andy Hardy films, starring Mickey Rooney, were hugely popular. Each movie featured Andy, America's favorite adolescent. As a middle-class high school student, Andy experiences all the

Ginger Rogers and Fred Astaire starred in several song-and-dance movies in the 1930s. The films' lavish sets and fairy-tale plots helped people forget about the Depression—for an hour or two.

typical teen traumas: dating, girls, first kisses, first jobs, and buying a car. The character created a wholesome teen image that young people and their parents embraced.

Judy Garland appeared with Mickey Rooney in several movies, and the two became teen sensations. In 1939 the pair toured the country together to promote Garland's starring role as Dorothy in *The Wizard of Oz*. Young people turned out in droves to see them. Garland and Rooney were mobbed by thousands of screaming fans wherever they went. Rooney received a special Academy Award in 1939 for his "significant contribution in bringing to the screen the spirit and personification of youth."

GOLDEN AGE OF RADIO

In the 1930s, the majority of American homes contained at least one radio. In the midst of the Depression, radio helped hold the nation together. President Roosevelt used radio to reach all Americans. In a series of broadcasts called fireside chats, Roosevelt explained his policies and programs and encouraged the American people.

Radio broadcasts were also an important means of escape. Families gathered around the big wooden box to listen for hours each day. "The radio occupied a prominent place at the end of the living room," recalled Joan Waller of Chicago. "Couch cushions on the floor provided seating as well as something soft to lie on while engrossed in daily radio episodes."

Teens enjoyed radio serials, programs in which story lines are carried from one episode to the next. Many serials had adventure themes about superheroes, cowboys, and space travelers. These included *The Adventures of Superman*, *The Cisco Kid*, and *Flash Gordon*. Often an episode ended with a thrilling scene called a cliffhanger. The cliffhangers left listeners not knowing what fate awaited their heroes. The suspense kept them tuning in. "As I stretched out listening to it, night after night . . . ," recalled Gerald Nachman, a teen in the 1930s, "the world seemed—sounded, rather—intimate, manageable, and coherent yet at the same time vast and mysterious and thrilling." Comedy shows were also popular with young people, as were, of course, music programs.

SWING!

Swing music was popular with teens in the 1930s, and the growth of the radio industry helped it gain popularity. Swing combined the jazz sounds of the 1920s with the powerful sound of an orchestra. Jazz orchestras were called big bands. Big band musicians William "Count" Basie, Jimmy Dorsey, Tommy Dorsey, Duke Ellington, Benny Goodman, and Glenn Miller were all masters of swing.

Teens spent hours listening to radio broadcasts of their favorite bands. They formed fan clubs, read *Down Beat* magazine, and learned all they could about swing musicians. On Saturday nights, they listened to *Your Hit Parade* to see if their favorite song reached number one on the charts. Jukeboxes were also introduced in the 1930s. These coin-operated phonographs helped make swing music easily accessible to young people.

Swing bands often performed in movie theaters to welcome the release of a new film and to boost ticket sales. Benny Goodman, known as the King of Swing, and his band performed at the Paramount Theater in Times Square, New York, on January 26, 1938. More than three thousand young people waited outside in the cold to get tickets. By the time the doors opened, the *Saturday Evening Post* reported, "Mr. Goodman's fans were multiplying by the minute, pouring up out of the Times Square subway exits like bees from a smoked hive."

The 3,664-seat theater sold out, and the theater managers called ten police officers to assist the ushers in handling the crowd. When Goodman appeared onstage and his band began to play, fans, "jumped up and down . . . they danced in the aisles, clambered upon the stage, waggled their hands, shook their shoulders, whinnied, whistled, clapped and sang." According to the *New York Times*, "It was a savage exhibition, as animalistic as a monkey's or an elephant's rhythmic swaying to the beat of a tom-tom [drum]."

Bandleader Cab Calloway *(center left)* appears in the short film *Hi-De-Ho* in the 1930s. Calloway wears a loose-fitting white zoot suit—a popular style for young African American and Latino men at the time.

In 1938 bandleader Cab Calloway published *The Hepster's Dictionary*. In it, Calloway provided a list of swing-related terms called jive talk. Swing musicians were called cats. They played git boxes (guitars) and skins (drums). A good dancer was a rug-cutter or a jitterbug. People who understood swing and jive were hepcats. People who didn't were squares or ickies.

Teens soon peppered their speech with this new language, leaving adults scratching their heads in confusion. Bound together by swing music and jive talk, young people were well on their way to establishing a national youth culture that went beyond class, race, and gender.

CHAPTER
FIVE

THE TEEN AGE

In September 1939, the army of German dictator Adolf Hitler, leader of the Nazi Party, invaded Poland. In the following months, in an attempt to take over Europe, the Nazis invaded Denmark, Norway, France, Belgium, Luxembourg, and the Netherlands. World War II (1939–1945) erupted as European nations fought back against the German army, its Nazi leadership, and its allies.

The United States sent weapons and supplies to its allies to fight Germany. But most Americans were against sending U.S. soldiers into the conflict. World War I had been deadly and devastating. Americans felt that another war abroad was not theirs to fight.

However, the United States would not be able to stay isolated. On December 7, 1941, Japan (a German ally) bombed the U.S. naval base at Pearl Harbor, Hawaii. The surprise attack killed more than two thousand U.S. citizens. It damaged or destroyed eight U.S. battleships. After Japan's attack, Americans changed their minds about entering the war. Pearl Harbor bound the country together with a shared purpose—to defeat Germany and Japan and their allies.

Many eighteen- and nineteen-year-old men enlisted in the armed forces. Some younger teens lied about their age and signed up as well. "At that age, you look forward to the glamour and have no idea of the horrors," explained one young man. "I wanted to be a hero," said another. "I was havin' trouble in school. I was havin' trouble with my mother. They didn't know what to do. I didn't wanna miss [the war]. . . . I was an American. I was seventeen."

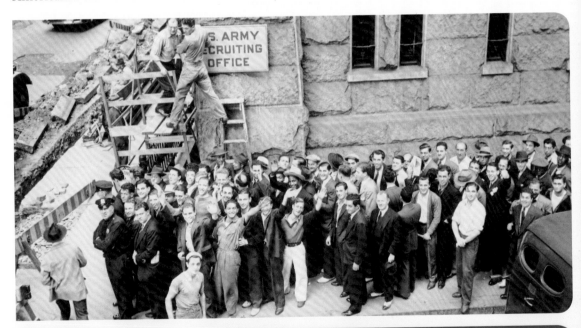

Young men line up to enlist in the U.S. Army in New York City in this early 1940s photo. More than 16 million Americans served in the armed forces in World War II. About 30 percent of male enlistees were age twenty and younger.

A woman checks artillery cartridges at an ammunition factory in Pennsylvania during World War II. Women and teens filled factory jobs left open when men went to war in Europe and the Pacific.

Gearing up for war pulled the United States out of the Depression. Factories needed workers to make weapons, ammunition, uniforms, tanks, ships, and airplanes. With so many men away fighting, factories were shorthanded. They hired women and teens of all races for jobs that were typically held by white men. Many states suspended their child labor laws during the war. Fourteen- to seventeen-year-olds became a valuable resource—necessary workers for the war machine.

Teens took on new responsibilities during the war. Some worked full-time. Others worked part-time while attending high school. In addition to working outside the home, many adolescents did the majority of household chores. "Some of us have younger sisters and brothers, and we not only have to do our home work but also have to prepare meals for the children, take care of them, help keep the house in order and see that there is food on the table when mother comes home from the factory," explained a girl from New York.

HIGH SCHOOL CONSUMERS

High school enrollment dropped during the war years as teens left school to work. Magazine and newspaper articles encouraged young people to stay in school and take their studies seriously. Adults urged students to think of getting a good education as their patriotic duty. The federal government also tried to keep adolescents in school. Through a series of films, pamphlets, and posters, the nation's leaders told young people to load up on math and science classes. Only an educated youth, claimed the government, would be able to handle the challenges of a world ravaged by war.

The war altered life for teens. Food shortages meant rationing (limiting supplies) of common items such as butter, sugar, meat, Coca-Cola, and chocolate. Even chewing gum became scarce.

Young people helped the war effort in a variety of ways. They held scrap drives and salvage campaigns. They collected tons of scrap items such as paper, metal, and rubber that could be recycled into war materials. They also raised millions of dollars to support the military.

High school students in the 1940s, like those of the previous decade, faced peer pressure to fit in and be popular at school. But unlike 1930s teens, young people in the 1940s had money to spend. Many worked at part-time jobs and earned their own spending money. Gasoline rationing meant no cars for cruising or for dates, and certain foods were scarce. But many teens could afford to buy clothes.

Girls wore belted dresses or skirts with clean, tailored lines. As fabric was needed for the war effort, skirts were slim and tailored to

To help with the war effort, these teens gather scrap metal from their neighborhood in California in 1942. The metal would be recycled to make guns and tanks.

Young women in the 1940s were expected to be feminine and wear skirts or dresses to school. These teens in Brooklyn, New York, protested the suspension of a fellow student—a young woman who wore pants to class—by also wearing trousers.

conserve material. Before the war, urban African American and Hispanic boys had been wearing zoot suits, baggy high-waisted pants with long wide-shouldered jackets. However, as the style grew in popularity, the government's War Production Board banned the making of zoot suits because they were considered a waste of valuable cloth.

High school students got the message that they needed to look a certain way, be a certain weight, and dress in certain acceptable styles. It was important to them to be part of a group and to act and speak and dress like their peers. Many teens believed that owning the right clothes would lead to popularity, dates, and happiness.

Clothing manufacturers, retailers, and advertisers targeted teen buyers for products designed specifically for them. Teen stores popped up all over the country, and department stores expanded their high school, or junior, departments. Advertisers promised high school girls sizes that fit their bodies and styles that fit their personalities. Companies also sold a huge array of beauty products—cosmetics, face cream, nail polish, perfume, and jewelry—all guaranteed to transform an ordinary high school girl into a beauty queen. Before long, a large-scale national market for teen clothing and accessories was firmly established and growing rapidly.

Girls read about the latest styles and clothing trends in fashion magazines. *Seventeen*, the first magazine for high school girls, hit newsstands in 1944. Its main focus was fashion, but it also included celebrity features; film, book, and record reviews; and advice on dating and how to handle parents. "SEVENTEEN is your magazine, High School Girls of America—all yours!" stated a 1944 article. "It is interested only in you—and in everything that concerns, excites, annoys, pleases or perplexes you." *Seventeen* was an instant hit. The first issue sold out in six days.

Thirteen- to nineteen-year-olds became a recognized economic force, and advertisers tried out new words to describe them. Some called them teeners or teensters. But the word that stuck, the word that quickly became the accepted definition of youth, was *teenager*.

HELLO, TEENAGER!

Teenagers in the 1940s enjoyed big bands and swing music. Eager to be distracted from war news, they listened to radio music, went to concerts and movies, and danced whenever they got the chance. They bought countless records, and swing music became central to teen culture. Teenage girls were particularly avid fans. Called bobby-soxers (because they wore short, folded white socks with saddle shoes or loafers), they listened to swing music for hours each day.

Swing fans danced the Lindy Hop (named after pilot Charles Lindbergh), the Suzie-Q, and the jitterbug. In these dances, the boy and girl danced separately, joined only by their right hands. Throughout the dance, they came together to twirl or spin. The boy sometimes tossed his partner into the air or slid her between his legs. Dancers made up steps as they went along. They jumped, jittered, and showed off their fancy footwork. Sometimes they showed off more than that. Bare-legged girls in twirling skirts revealed a lot of thigh and sometimes glimpses of panties in the lively dances.

Like parents of previous generations, adults worried about the effect of all this dancing on the moral character of their children. Some adults, such as Francis Beckman, the Catholic archbishop of Dubuque, Iowa, called swing music and jitterbugging evil. "We permit jam sessions, jitterbug . . . rhythm orgies to occupy a place in our social scheme of things, wooing our youth along the primrose path to hell," he wrote.

Swing music produced America's first teen idol—Frank Sinatra. Sinatra was a young singer from Hoboken, New Jersey, when he signed with the Tommy Dorsey Band in the 1940s. Sinatra soon left the band and launched a solo singing career. Bobby-soxers fell in love with the thin, good-looking crooner. Known as the Voice, Sinatra was famous for his soft, mellow singing. He sang love songs and ballads filled with loneliness,

A couple takes part in a swing dance contest in 1946. Swing partners often danced far apart to allow room for fast footwork, twirls, and jumps.

longing, and unrequited love. His popular recordings of the period include "I'll Never Smile Again," "Saturday Night (Is the Loneliest Night of the Week)," and "I Dream of You."

Bobby-soxers mobbed Sinatra wherever he went. Thousands of teenage girls stood in line for hours to buy tickets to his concerts. Some of them skipped school to hear him sing. They wore bow ties, because Frank did, and pinned his picture to their dresses. When Sinatra took the stage, his fans screamed, sometimes so loudly that they drowned out the music. They moaned, wept, and fainted. They threw roses on the stage. Some of them also threw their panties and bras. Ushers carried bottles of ammonia to revive fans who had fainted. An ambulance sat outside the theater, just in case it was needed to whisk an overwrought teenager to the hospital.

Sinatra also had a few male teenage fans. Some boys, however, jealous of all the screaming, swooning adoration, threw raw eggs at him during concerts. Others threw ripe tomatoes at the singer's theater marquee photographs. But that didn't stop the bobby-soxers. They followed Sinatra like the Pied Piper. Adults feared this mass hysteria and worried where the idol worship would lead their children. A member of Congress called Sinatra, "the prime instigator of juvenile delinquency in America."

Bobby-soxers and reporters mob singer Frank Sinatra as he gets off a train in Pasadena, California, in the 1940s. Sinatra is often considered America's first teen idol.

RISE OF JUVENILE CRIME

With fathers off fighting a war and mothers working in factories producing war goods, teenagers had less parental supervision during the mid-1940s. Juvenile crime exploded, and courts were filled with young offenders. Complaints included vandalism, auto theft, and teenage petting and drinking parties. "You see it in the papers every day," stated *Look* magazine, "five boys caught stealing automobiles; a 15-year-old girl charged with 30 sex offenses; in Detroit, a juvenile mob invades night clubs, bars, movies, smashing windows and furniture; in Los Angeles, a gang of boys requires new members to have seduced a girl, or stolen; a father reproves [scolds] his 17-year-old son, and the next day the father's mutilated body is found beside a railroad track."

Juvenile delinquents represented a tiny slice of the total teen population. But the frequency and severity of their crimes shocked adults. Media coverage of teenage crime increased, and countless stories appeared in magazines and newspapers. The focus on young offenders elevated the juvenile crime problem to a national crisis. All over the country, teenagers seemed out of control. Parents worried that delinquency was no longer a problem found only in lower-class neighborhoods and back alleys. Middle-class teens—the "good kids" in high school—also got into trouble. They disrupted school events, talked back to their parents and teachers, and showed no respect for their elders. J. Edgar Hoover, the director of the Federal Bureau of Investigation (or FBI, a government agency that investigates crime), warned Americans that "this country is in deadly peril. A creeping rot of moral disintegration is eating into our nation."

Some experts blamed comic books, movies, and swing music for the increase in juvenile crime. The majority, however, blamed irresponsible parents. They complained that mothers worked full-time and left their teenagers to fend for themselves. They claimed that parents failed to discipline their children, and as a result, children did not respect rules. "The biggest trouble with children these days," wrote the *Indianapolis News*, "is that instead of doing what their parents tell them to do, they tell their parents what to do, and the parents do it. So what else can you expect but a generation of saucy, independent, reckless youngsters."

Some communities imposed curfews to keep teenagers off the streets at night. But high school students did not want to give up Friday night football games or Saturday night dances. They complained loudly and bitterly against the rules.

In 1944 teen canteens, or neighborhood recreation centers, opened in cities and towns all across the country. Located in YMCA rooms, churches, and community centers, teen canteens were designed to keep high school students off the streets and out of trouble. They provided teenagers a safe place where they could hang out together, listen to music, and dance without intrusive adult supervision. With names such as Jive Hive, Buzz Bucket, Boogie Barn, or Hep Cat Hall, teen canteens contained Ping-Pong tables, a jukebox, a dance floor, and a snack bar.

A group of boys get tough on a New York City street in 1942. The 1940s saw a rise in juvenile crime, leading to new restrictions on teen activities.

World War II ended in the summer of 1945 with an allied victory. Fathers returned home from military service, and mothers quit their jobs outside the home. But life did not settle back into the old patterns of prewar days. Teenagers had grown into a separate and distinct group in society. They had their own youth culture, and the gap widened between teens and their parents. Teenagers had enjoyed a great deal of unsupervised freedom during the war years. And just because Mom and Dad were back home, teens had no plans to give that freedom back.

*I've got a bad reputation and
I'm going to live up to it.*

—EDDIE, FOURTEEN, WASHINGTON, D.C., 1953

CHAPTER SIX

ROCK AND ROLL

World War II revived the U.S. economy. After years of anxiety and hardship, Americans looked forward to a bright future. Many benefited from a surge of economic prosperity.

The government began a program, called the G.I. Bill, to help returning soldiers readjust to civilian life. Millions of veterans used money from the G.I. Bill to start or continue their education or job training. This paved the way for them to get high-paying jobs. Other veterans used G.I. Bill money to start their own businesses.

Large numbers of veterans also used low-interest government loans to buy homes. Across the country, many families (especially white families) were able to leave crowded city housing. They moved to the suburbs—often new communities on the outskirts of towns and cities. People regarded the suburbs as open and clean, with less traffic, less noise, and less crime than inner cities. Suburbs had more green space—lawns, trees, and flowers—and better services, including better schools. To meet the demands of these new suburban residents, builders erected thousands of inexpensive houses of similar design.

Built between 1947 and 1951, Levittown, New York, was one of the first suburbs in the United States constructed to house the expanding U.S. population after World War II.

The United States emerged as a superpower after World War II. So did the Union of Soviet Socialist Republics (USSR). A period of tense relations between the West (the United States and its Allies) and the USSR set in. The West was democratic and embraced the free market (an economy with little government regulation). The USSR was Communist. Communism is a system that relies on heavy government regulation of the political process and the economy. Each side wanted to be more powerful, economically and militarily, than the other. The period was known as the Cold War (1945–1991), because it did not involve any direct battles between the United States and the USSR. But the fear of a "hot" war breaking out, in which nuclear weapons would be used, was real and intense.

Nevertheless, with good jobs and new homes, many Americans felt a strong sense of well-being and security. Many couples chose to have large families. The result was a baby boom—a huge increase in births. More than 76 million babies were born in the United States during the postwar baby boom (1946–1964). Those baby boomers, along with the nation's economic prosperity, fueled a revolution in teen culture.

SPENDING BILLIONS IN THE BURBS

Many middle-class teenagers in the 1950s received an allowance from their parents and also worked at part-time jobs. With their parents doing well financially, these teens were not expected to turn over their wages to help the family. Their money was their own to spend on things other than necessities—it was disposable income.

Baby boomers filled U.S. schools in the 1950s. This gymnasium at a high school in Midwest City, Oklahoma, was used for many different classes at one time to accommodate the large number of students in the school.

A young entrepreneur named Eugene Gilbert realized the vast potential of teenage buyers with disposable incomes. He also knew that many businesses had no idea what teens liked and were interested in. Gilbert hired high school students to interview other teenagers and identify their tastes. The pollsters found out what products teenagers used and what products they wanted to buy. Gilbert then sold the information to manufacturers and advertising agencies.

Gilbert's success launched an entire industry of teen market research companies. They monitored teenage preferences in everything from shoes to toothpaste. The research showed that peer opinions were more important to teenagers than adult opinions. Research also showed that teenagers not only spent their own money on products they chose, but they influenced their parents' buying habits as well. According to journalist Richard Gehman, "They are responsible for so many decisions we make, they influence so many of our purchases, they inspire so many designs and styles and institute so many fads, that it is possible to regard them as a vast, determined band of blue-jeaned storm troopers [soldiers], forcing us all to do exactly as they dictate."

Teenagers became the primary sales target for all kinds of products. Manufacturers depended on them to buy snack foods, soft drinks, acne creams, magazines, typewriters, transistor radios, phonograph record players, and countless other products. "These days, merchants eye teenagers the way stockmen eye cattle," wrote Dwight MacDonald in the *New Yorker* magazine in 1958. But advertisers and merchants did not target all teens. They sought white buyers. Minority teenagers were not yet a recognized part of the growing teen market.

Starting in the 1950s, teenagers—especially white teenagers—became the primary target of advertisers selling snack foods, soft drinks such as Canada Dry Ginger Ale *(above)*, and other products.

Clothing designed for teenagers became big business. Girls wore dresses or skirts that fell below the knee with blouses or sweaters to school and on dates. Full skirts made of felt (sometimes appliquéd with poodles) were also popular, as were round-collared blouses worn under sweaters. For leisure wear, girls wore rolled-up jeans with blouses or with men's shirts. They wore flat shoes—penny loafers or saddle shoes—with white bobby socks.

White teenage boys in the 1950s had two primary styles: clean cut or greaser. Clean-cut boys wore chinos (plain cotton trousers) or khakis with a belt. They paired the trousers with cotton shirts with button-down collars. They cut their hair short and straight across the top—a flattop. Greasers wore tight black or blue rolled-up jeans with white T-shirts. They often rolled up the sleeves of their shirts to show off their biceps. They also stored their cigarettes in the fold of the sleeve. Greasers slicked back their hair with petroleum jelly or oil into a ducktail and kept combs in their pockets to sweep stray locks into place.

SEPARATE BUT NOT EQUAL

The vast majority of teenagers in the 1950s attended high school. But most schools were racially segregated, or separated. African Americans went to black schools, and white students went to white schools. Some black students had to pass white schools on the way to their black school. Public schools were supposed to be "separate but equal," but the schools for white students were usually far superior. Many white schools had modern buildings, new textbooks, top-notch teachers, and advanced classes. Black students studied from worn-out books in crumbling facilities.

In 1954 the U.S. Supreme Court ruled on a case called *Brown v. Board of Education.* The ruling stated that it was unconstitutional for states to run racially segregated public schools. The court stated that school segregation deprived African American children of equal educational opportunities. "Separate educational facilities are inherently unequal," wrote U.S. chief justice Earl Warren.

Many schools in the South resisted the ruling. White segregationists fought to keep African Americans out of white schools. In 1957 violence broke out in schools all across the South. In Little Rock, Arkansas, Governor Orval Faubus ordered the Arkansas National Guard troops to surround the all-white Central High School and block black students from entering the building. In Birmingham, Alabama, an angry mob of racists shouted obscenities and beat African American students who tried to enter a white high school.

Teenagers watched these events unfold on television. They saw the contradiction between what the Constitution said about freedom and the reality of inequality for African Americans in the United States. Many teenagers, both black and white, began to think about prejudice in new ways and to question its place in a democratic nation.

African American students gradually began to attend formerly all-white high schools. But these early freedom fighters did not have an easy time. Black students were not allowed to play on white sports teams. They could not join the school band or go to the senior prom. Racist students often harassed, taunted, and tried to force blacks out of "their" schools. White students who talked to or befriended blacks were often ostracized by their peers. Some of them received threatening phone calls or hate mail.

School integration eventually paid off. Whites and blacks

Elizabeth Eckford (in white shirt at right) is verbally attacked by white students while entering Central High School in Little Rock, Arkansas, in 1957. Eckford and eight other African American students were the first to integrate Central High. The students became known as the Little Rock Nine.

learned from each other and taught their elders important lessons about tolerance. "Senior year I asked this white guy if he'd sign my yearbook," said Arlam Carr, an African American student in Montomery, Alabama, in the 1950s. "I had known him from the tenth grade on, and we had become pretty good friends. He wrote that at one time he had been a bigot and had hated black people. Now he realized that people are people, black or white. Meeting me and knowing me had changed him."

CRUISIN'

Most middle-class American families owned a car in the 1950s. Borrowing the family car for a night out gave teenagers an easy way to be alone with a date or to meet up with a group of friends. Some teenagers bought their own cars. Magazines such as *Hot Rod* helped teens (mostly boys) transform run-down jalopies (old cars) into symbols of teen cool. In 1955 Chevrolet marketed a "hot car"—with a powerful V-8 engine—to teenagers. Drag racing (a race run on a straight course, such as a street) became a popular activity in some cities. Because of the dangers of this craze, car insurance rates for drivers below the age of twenty-five skyrocketed.

Teenagers often cruised around town with their friends. On a typical evening, they dropped by the local drive-in restaurant or soda shop. They listened to music on the jukebox and danced. They ate hamburgers with mounds of fries and drank milk shakes or root beer floats. But food was not the primary motivation for going to these hangouts. Teens wanted to see their friends, flirt with potential dates, see, and be seen.

Drive-in movies were also popular in the 1950s. Teenagers parked their cars in front of a giant movie screen and hooked individual speakers onto their car windows. Parents worried that their teenagers were doing more at the drive-in than watching a movie. They feared that drive-ins were "passion pits with pix"—perfect places for sexual experimentation. As a result of this parental concern, some drive-ins hired guards to stroll past each car, peek in through the windows, and "prevent any sort of misconduct."

THE BOX

By the 1950s, millions of Americans owned televisions. The first TVs had picture screens between 10 and 15 inches (25 to 38 cm) wide diagonally, inside a large, heavy cabinet. Broadcasts were in black and white until 1954, when RCA introduced the first television to broadcast in color.

Most households had only one TV, and it became the center of family life for many people. They watched anything that aired. TV dinners and TV trays were new products that allowed family members to eat in the living room while watching their favorite programs, instead of around a table in the dining room or the kitchen. In many families, teens and their parents gave up chances for daily conversation as everyone sat glued to "the box."

Teenagers watched family shows such as *The Adventures of Ozzie and Harriet*, *Father Knows Best*, *Make Room for Daddy*, and *Leave It to Beaver*. These programs showed suburban, white, middle-class families with two or three children. They had wise and patient dads and stay-at-home moms. Each of these shows portrayed teenagers as clean-cut and happy-go-lucky. This format was in keeping with the guidelines of the National Association of Broadcasters. Stations agreed never to air programs or commercials that might "break down juvenile respect for parents, the home or moral conduct."

Another popular TV show, *American Bandstand*, was a huge hit among young people. Billed as a dance party, the show aired five days a week to an estimated twenty million viewers. Teenagers hurried home from school to hear the latest popular songs and learn the latest dance steps. *American Bandstand* had a regular cast of teenage dancers. Viewers knew the dancers' names, and the Bandstand Kids became teenage celebrities.

American Bandstand provided a wholesome image of teenagers. Boys wore coats and ties, while girls wore dresses or skirts and blouses. Girls were not allowed to wear tight sweaters, low-cut blouses, or slacks. They also followed a code of behavior to set a good example for their fans. *American Bandstand* was one of the first television programs to present

Bandstand (above) started in 1952 as a local Philadelphia, Pennsylvania, music and dance TV show. The television network ABC took over the show in 1957. Renamed *American Bandstand*, the show was broadcast nationally.

a racially mixed view of teenagers. African American and Latino couples danced alongside white couples. But the partners never mixed.

TEEN PICS

The popularity of television hurt the movie industry. Many adults stopped going to movies. They preferred to stay home and watch TV. To boost ticket sales, moviemakers studied audiences in the early 1950s to see who attended movies and who did not. They discovered that teenagers went to movies more often than adults. Teens enjoyed the experience of sitting in the dark with friends or with a date watching a movie on a large screen. For them, it was a social event.

Hollywood cashed in on this trend by making movies with characters teenagers could identify with. Many were films about troubled teens and juvenile delinquents. *Rebel Without a Cause* (1955) became the classic delinquent film of the era. In a raw performance, young actor James Dean played the role of Jim Stark, a lonely teenager trying to fit in at a new high school. Stark is tormented by his parents' marital problems and a hostile school environment. He teeters on the brink of delinquency and struggles to find his place among adults and among his peers. Jim finds friendship with two equally lonely teens—Judy (Natalie Wood) and Plato (Sal Mineo). The film portrays an upper-middle-class community divided—teenagers on one side, parents on the other.

Teenagers adored James Dean. Girls felt they understood his sensitive soul. Boys imitated his image as a rebellious loner. Many teenagers embraced the star's philosophy of life: "Dream as if you'll live forever. Live as if you'll die today." When James Dean died in a car accident on September 30, 1955, at the age of twenty-four, he became a teen icon. Thousands of fans traveled to his hometown of Fairmount, Indiana, for his funeral.

The box office success of *Rebel* led to a whole genre of movies, called teenpics, designed to attract a young audience. The 1956 film *Rock Around the Clock* was the first hugely successful teenpic. In the film, band promoter Steve Hollis stumbles upon a Saturday night dance in a small town. The dance features the band Bill Haley and the Comets. "What is that outfit playing up there?" Hollis wonders. "It isn't boogie, it isn't jive, and it isn't swing. It's kind of all of them." A dancer in the crowd answers, "It's rock 'n' roll, brother, and we're rocking tonight!" The film introduced rock-and-roll music to a worldwide audience. It also proved that movies targeted to teenagers could be extremely profitable. Teenpics became big business.

ELVIS!

Bill Haley and the Comets was just one of the early rock-and-roll bands to gain popularity in the 1950s. Early rock and roll combined rhythm and blues (or R & B, a traditionally African American form of popular music) and country music (popular with southern whites). Black radio stations played the R & B music of Ray Charles, Fats Domino, B. B. King, Chuck Berry, and other African American singers. White teenagers began to listen to the music too, on late night radio programs

Rebel Without a Cause (1955) is a classic teen movie—it shows teens who have family problems, fall in love, are bullied, and find friendship.

Elvis Presley took his rock-and-roll stardom to the big screen in the 1950s. This still is from the 1956 movie *Love Me Tender*.

when their parents were asleep. Young people, both black and white, could not get enough of the sound.

Elvis Presley, a young white man from Tupelo, Mississippi, took the black R & B sound and brought it into mainstream pop culture as rock and roll. The nation's first rock-and-roll superstar, Presley had a distinctive voice and sang with unexpected rhythms. He swiveled his hips and moved in sexually suggestive ways. He looked tough, confident, and full of raw energy. And his music drove teenagers wild. In 1956 alone, Presley sold more than ten million records.

Ed Sullivan, the host of America's most popular variety show, saw Presley perform. Sullivan said he would never invite Presley to sing on his show because Presley's hip-swiveling dance moves were far too suggestive for television. Sullivan soon changed his mind. Presley was a national sensation, too popular to ignore. He appeared on *The Ed Sullivan Show* three times. However, he was only filmed from the waist up to make sure America's morals stayed intact. Sullivan's television ratings went through the roof.

THE TEEN SOUND

Rock and roll was defined by an insistent, unmistakable beat. Wailing electric guitars got teenagers up and dancing. According to one music executive, teenagers liked the music "for the same reason they like to ride motorcycles. It moves and it's exciting, and who cares if there's a lotta noise."

Rock-and-roll lyrics celebrated the everyday experiences of teenagers: dating, problems with parents, high school, and first love. The sound quickly gained popularity with teens from coast to coast. Movie sound tracks included rock-and-roll songs. Rock radio stations grew in number. Inexpensive transistor radios allowed teenagers to listen to music any time of the day or night. Record sales exploded. Teenagers bought long-playing records (LPs) that contained several songs on a two-sided disc—up to twenty-three minutes on each side of uninterrupted music. Teens also bought small records called 45s for as little as sixty-nine cents apiece. Most 45s contained two songs—one on each side of the disc. The 45s could be stacked ten at a time on the spindle of a record player.

Rock and roll differed from other types of music because it was created for and marketed to teenagers. As the music grew in popularity, many adults thought rock and roll would lead to loose morals and rotted minds. Middle-class parents feared that rock and roll and teenage rebel culture would infect their children. They cited the growing juvenile crime statistics as proof that teenagers were out of control. Magazines and newspapers fueled adult panic by depicting urban teenagers as switchblade-toting thugs. The level of crime was not as great as the media made it out to be, but these reports increased the perception of juvenile crime as part of teenage life.

All across the country, some adults tried to stop the spread of rock and roll. Some cities banned rock-and-roll concerts or dances. Others did not allow the music to be played on the radio. But rock could not be stopped. By the late 1950s, teenagers bought more than 70 percent of all records. This accounted for more than $50 million in yearly sales, with millions more from related products such as phonographs.

Adult reaction to rock and roll illuminated the growing distance between teenagers and their parents. The more their parents protested, the more teenagers listened to rock and roll. This rebellion was one of the forces that set the stage for teenage political activism in the 1960s and 1970s.

Teens listen to 45s (small records) on a phonograph in the 1950s. Teenaged consumers played a huge part in the rise of rock and roll. They bought records, phonographs, radios, and magazines featuring their favorite musicians.

CHAPTER
SEVEN

A CULTURE
OF DISCONTENT

By 1960 the first children born during the postwar baby boom had reached their teen years. The U.S. teenage population grew dramatically. Nearly half the population was under the age of twenty-five. Middle-class teenagers in the 1960s did not grow up with food shortages as Depression-era teens had. They had no first-hand knowledge of the sacrifices required of a nation at war. A strong economy meant that most teens grew up with more money, possessions, and opportunities than any previous generation.

Teenagers in the 1960s were better educated than their parents. They had high hopes for the future and a strong sense of their own importance as a group. They believed they could make a difference in the world.

They believed their actions mattered to society. "I always had a sense that our generation was bigger and better than any that had come before," said one man who had grown up in the era. "And probably bigger and better than any that would follow. Every time we turned around, something was happening that we felt we had control over. We had the feeling that somehow we were the chosen. We were gonna make the world right."

President John F. Kennedy took office in 1961. At forty-three years old, he was the youngest elected U.S. president. In his inaugural address, Kennedy spoke to the nation's youth. "The torch has been passed to a new generation of Americans," he told them. The president challenged teenagers to get involved and help make a better America for all. He inspired hope and optimism. Teenagers identified with the charismatic leader and were eager to answer the call. "I really believed that I was going to be able to change the world," said one sixteen-year-old girl.

On November 22, 1963, while visiting Dallas, Texas, Kennedy was assassinated by a gunman named Lee Harvey Oswald. The sudden, senseless violence

As the youngest elected U.S. president, John F. Kennedy represented a new American era to many people. His assassination in 1963 devastated the country.

stunned the nation. Many young people, such as New Yorker Jeff Greenfield, took Kennedy's death personally. Teenagers lost their optimism, and their shared grief bound them together as a group. "To understand that this supremely confident, self-assured man could be slaughtered in broad daylight, his head blown off by some madman (or by some sinister conspiracy; no one could be sure) was to understand the fragility of life, the powerful forces lurking just under the surface of life. What our parents learned in a war, or in a struggle for survival, we learned that November. No one was safe; if not John Kennedy, then definitely not any of us."

Stevie Wonder was the stage name of Stevland Hardaway Morris, shown here in 1963. Blind since birth, Wonder was a young teen when he became a hit-maker for Detroit's Motown record label.

THE BEAT GOES ON

Music helped teenagers heal, and the 1960s was a decade for music lovers. Rock and roll expanded to include a variety of different sounds. The Beach Boys had a string of hit songs about Southern California, surfing, fast cars, pretty girls, beach parties, and romance. Teenagers loved the light, breezy songs and perfectly blended voices. The music made young people want to hop in their cars, cruise to the beach, catch a wave, and party.

Soul music and R & B expanded in the 1960s. Owned and operated by African Americans, Motown Record Corporation in Detroit, Michigan, launched the careers of many African American musicians. Motown's stars included Diana Ross and the Supremes, Marvin Gaye, Stevie Wonder, and the Temptations. These musicians faced discrimination when they performed, especially in the South. But people of all races enjoyed their music and bought their records. Their talent broke barriers and expanded white teenage popular culture to include African Americans. The music empowered blacks as they struggled for equal rights.

American pop music of the era ranged from California beach music to Detroit soul. But in the mid-1960s, a whole new dimension was added by artists from Great Britain. Dubbed the British Invasion, this influx of pop music included the Who, the Zombies, the Rolling Stones, and the Kinks. Leading the invasion were four young men from Liverpool, England—the Beatles.

The Beatles—Paul McCartney, John Lennon, Ringo Starr, and George Harrison—sang pop ballads and catchy tunes. The young men were good looking, funny, and appealing. By the time the band arrived in New York for a U.S. tour in February 1964, Beatlemania was in full swing. When they performed on *The Ed Sullivan Show* on February 9, almost half the country watched. American teenagers went wild. Boys grew their hair long to imitate the Beatles' style. Girls joined Beatles fan clubs and doodled "I love Paul" on their notebooks. The band had six number one songs in 1964.

Teenagers loved the Beatles' hair and clothing styles and their cheeky wit as much as they loved the music. The Beatles' boyish enthusiasm was contagious. Many parents also liked the Beatles. They were modern without being threatening. "They look beat-up and depraved in the nicest possible way," wrote one reporter.

As the decade wore on, the Beatles' music came to reflect the social and political changes sweeping the nation. Instead of singing "I Want to Hold Your Hand," they sang "Revolution," and other songs of political protest. Bob Dylan became the most influential of a group of folk artists who also wrote protest songs. These artists challenged the status quo and questioned establishment values. Dylan's songs, such as "Blowin' in the Wind" and "The Times They Are a-Changin'" were about civil rights, poverty, and war. He inspired teenagers to speak out against injustice and become active in their communities. Dylan was one of a number of folksingers who made teenagers believe they could solve the nation's problems if they worked together.

Two teenage girls excitedly await the arrival of the Beatles in New York in 1964. Beatlemania lasted throughout the rest of the 1960s and into the early 1970s.

THE FIGHT FOR RIGHTS

One of the things teenagers protested in the 1960s was racial segregation. In the South, "whites-only" restaurants, water fountains, movie theaters, and public restrooms were still the norm. African Americans could not swim in whites-only pools or use whites-only libraries. They had to sit at the back of the bus and give up their seats to white passengers.

Several leaders emerged from African American communities to lead demonstrations against segregation and racial injustice. Martin Luther King Jr., in particular, rose to national prominence with his nonviolent approach to campaigning for civil rights. King believed that marches, sit-ins (peacefully occupying an area, such as a building, during a demonstration), and boycotts (refusing to do business with certain stores and companies) would bring positive media attention to the civil rights movement. Such nonviolent acts would show that the movement was organized and dignified and would gain the movement public sympathy. A powerful public speaker, King inspired many Americans.

African American teens peacefully demonstrated at segregated lunch counters, bus stations, and movie theaters. They waded into segregated pools and prayed at all-white churches. They faced violence and were often hauled off to jail. White teenagers saw blacks beaten and arrested. In sympathy and solidarity, many of them joined the civil rights movement.

With pressure from the younger generation, the times did begin to change. Congress passed three landmark civil rights bills in 1964, 1965, and 1968. The new laws banned discrimination in public places, employment, voting, and housing. But the civil rights movement

In August 1963, about 300,000 people gathered in Washington, D.C., for the March on Washington, a political rally in support of civil rights. At the rally, Martin Luther King Jr. *(above)* delivered his historic "I Have a Dream" speech about racial equality.

suffered a terrible set-back in 1968. On April 4, King was assassinated by a sniper in Memphis, Tennessee. As with Kennedy's death, King's murder was a blow to the optimism of the country's young people.

WHAT ARE WE FIGHTING FOR?

The United States sent combat troops to Vietnam in 1965. Communist North Vietnam was fighting non-Communist South Vietnam. U.S. soldiers fought alongside

Young African Americans protest segregation at a lunch counter in Memphis, Tennessee, in 1961. A white employee of the restaurant bars their way. Peaceful demonstrations such as this were part of the American civil rights movement led by Martin Luther King Jr.

the South Vietnamese in an attempt to stop the spread of Communism. In previous wars, battles and other events had been reported in newspapers and movie newsreels. But television brought the Vietnam War (1957–1975) directly into American homes. For the first time in history, teenagers watched the grisly scenes of war from their living rooms. Images of children and other civilians injured by bombs, of dead bodies piled up after battles, of tired and discouraged soldiers, deeply affected America's young people. Many teenagers thought the Vietnam War was immoral and unjust. Young men also faced being drafted as soldiers when they turned eighteen.

In 1965 three high school students in Des Moines, Iowa, wore black armbands to school to protest the Vietnam War. They were suspended from school. The students argued that the Free Speech Clause of the First

Siblings Mary Beth and John Tinker hold the protest armbands that caused their suspension from school in 1965. Four years later, the U.S. Supreme Court ruled that their peaceful protest of the Vietnam War was within their constitutional rights.

Amendment to the U.S Constitution allowed them to peacefully express their views. In 1969 the U.S. Supreme Court agreed. In *Tinker v. Des Moines Independent School System*, the Court ruled that students have free speech rights in public schools as long as they do not disrupt the educational process.

This landmark decision led to greater freedom of expression in school newspapers and journals. It was part of a national trend to expand the rights of young people. In another landmark decision, the Supreme Court also ruled about the rights of teenagers during juvenile delinquency proceedings. The court case called *In re Gault* (1967) ruled that teens being tried in juvenile courts must be given the same basic rights and protections as adults accused of crimes.

DO YOUR OWN THING

In the 1960s, many college-age people rejected the values of their parents. They refused to accept social injustice as "just the way things are." They did not believe that success equaled a house full of expensive possessions. Instead, they looked for ways to create a less violent society with more individual freedoms. Students protested on college campuses. They began to "drop out" of normal society. They smoked marijuana and took LSD, a powerful mind-altering drug. Young men grew long hair and beards. Young women stopped wearing bras and girdles. Some young people left school and formed communes—communities where people lived together, sharing money and resources. Their slogan became, "If it feels good, do it." The press called them hippies.

The media bombarded society with images of hippies. The hippie lifestyle captured the imagination of high school students. The development of the birth control pill gave females an effective control over pregnancy, and the number of sexually active high school students increased. Marijuana use also increased among teens. Teenagers began to openly challenge their parents. Adults coined the term *generation gap* to refer to the gulf that stretched between teenagers and adults.

Teenage fashion in the 1960s reflected youth's desire to "do your own thing." The mod (short for "modern") style originated in London, England, and was very popular in the early 1960s. Mod girls wore miniskirts that fell about 8 inches (20 cm) above the knee. Girls also favored bright colors, wildly printed fabrics, stripes, sparkles, beads, and flowers. They finished off their outfits with brightly colored tights, flat shoes or knee-high boots, and huge hoop earrings. Their makeup included pale foundation (for white girls), white lipstick, and false eyelashes. Mod boys wore paisley shirts, striped pants, pointy boots, and wide ties.

The hippie style became popular later in the decade. Hippies favored natural fabrics and ethnic (for example, African or Indian) designs. Hippie girls wore low-riding bell-bottom pants and jeans. The pants were often paired with loose, embroidered peasant blouses. Hippie boys also wore jeans with tie-dyed T-shirts under fringed leather vests. Beads, peace symbols, rings, flowers, colored sunglasses, and sandals were popular with both sexes. Many African American teens grew

In this 1966 photo, British fashion model Twiggy wears a mod ensemble—miniskirt, flat shoes, carefully styled hair, and heavy eye makeup.

their hair in natural Afros, while white, Latino, and Native American teens wore their hair long and unstyled.

High school officials and teenagers clashed over clothing styles and hair lengths. According to school rules, boys wore their hair too long and girls wore their skirts too short. Many students challenged school dress codes and convinced school districts around the country to abolish or ease their codes. "I believe a teen-ager, or anyone else, will act basically the same no matter what he has on," explained a high school girl from Indiana. "It is not the clothes, but the person inside those clothes, that matters."

INTO THE '70S

The political activism of teenagers in the 1960s resulted in some important changes. In 1971 Congress passed the Twenty-sixth Amendment to the Constitution. The amendment made eighteen the standard voting age in all U.S. states. Previously, states could set their own minimum voting ages. The amendment was significant because eighteen-year-old men were being drafted to serve in the Vietnam War. Voting gave them a political voice.

In 1973 the United States signed the Paris Peace Accords. The treaty ended U.S. military involvement in the Vietnam War. U.S. troops began withdrawing from Vietnam.

Later that year, Vice President Spiro Agnew resigned. He had been charged with accepting bribes and falsifying federal tax returns when he was governor of Maryland. President Richard Nixon also became embroiled in a scandal called Watergate. People in the Nixon administration had been caught spying on and trying to sabotage political opponents. The scandal centered on a break-in at the Democratic Party's national headquarters at the Watergate Hotel in Washington, D.C. In 1973 investigators found that President Nixon had authorized the break-in and other illegal actions. Congress moved to impeach (bring formal charges against) Nixon. Instead, on August 9, 1974, Nixon resigned—the first president in U.S. history to do so. The loss in Vietnam coupled with the scandals in Washington caused many teenagers to lose faith in the government. They felt the government could not be trusted.

SLUMPING SCORES

Despite the "do your own thing" spirit of the time, high school students still divided into social groups and cliques. Students typically fell into one of several roles—for example, jock, weirdo, popular girl, bad boy, and nerd. Members of each group dressed and acted their part. "You do have to change yourself if you want friends," said a high school student named Sarah. "Because, no matter what anybody says, peer pressure is there, and you have to follow it to survive. . . . It's not a very idealistic thing . . . you are supposed to be yourself, you're supposed to be an individual. There are few people who can dare do that."

President Richard Nixon announces his resignation on TV on August 8, 1974. The Watergate scandal that led to Nixon's resignation embittered many Americans' view of government.

Educators experimented with all kinds of new programs to help students learn. High schools in the 1970s created open classrooms, common areas, and more relaxed dress codes. Students could choose a wider variety of electives, such as psychology, photography, filmmaking, and African American history. However, scores for college-bound students on the Scholastic Aptitude Test (SAT) dropped steadily in the 1970s. Fewer students graduated from high school. Educators were baffled and searched for causes. Former Secretary of Labor Willard Wirtz and a twenty-one-member committee studied the problem for two years.

Their report found that high school students in the 1970s were less serious about their studies than earlier generations of teenagers. They also discovered that many students no longer read for enjoyment. "We never

Two *Soul Train* dancers pose in Los Angeles, California, in 1974. *Soul Train* began as a local Chicago TV program in 1970. The next year, it reached national audiences. *Soul Train* was the first TV show geared toward a young African American audience. Its advertisers also saw the potential for reaching young black consumers.

had to read," said Joyce Maynard. "There was always TV, and so we grew accustomed to having our pictures presented to us, our characters described on the screen more satisfactorily, it seemed to many of us, than five pages of adjectives."

These discoveries set off a back-to-basics movement in high school education. Many educators cut back on music and art programs and focused on core subjects such as reading and math.

GIRL POWER

Throughout history, women have had fewer career options than men. In 1970 they earned 45 percent less than men for the same jobs. Women fought for equal rights in the 1970s. They wanted equal pay for equal work. They also wanted to be able to choose any career, and not just become a teacher, secretary, or nurse. The fight for equal rights spilled into America's high schools. Many teenage girls wanted to play team sports. But their opportunities were limited. Most high schools did not offer sports programs for girls.

In 1972 the U.S. government attempted to correct this situation. Congress passed Title IX of the Education Amendments. This law forced public schools to give girls the same opportunities to play team sports as boys. Many schools created girls' sports programs, and before long, teenage girls were playing baseball, basketball, volleyball, and soccer on high school teams.

Title IX of the Education Amendments forced schools to offer equal sports opportunities to boys and girls. Across the United States, girls took advantage of the new law and began playing sports such as basketball.

THE BIRTH OF THE BLOCKBUSTER

Filmmakers continued to look for new ways to lure teenagers away from their TVs and into movie theaters. Their answer was the blockbuster—a big expensive movie, often with a star cast and the best special effects of the day. In the summer of 1975, *Jaws* became a must-see blockbuster. Teenagers cringed in horror as a great white shark with a taste for humans terrorized a New England beach community. The movie raked in profits. It was the most successful film in the world up to that time and the first film to earn more than $100,000 at the box office.

Two years later, another blockbuster shattered *Jaws*'s record as top moneymaker. Teenagers stood in long lines to get tickets for *Star Wars*, a science-fiction epic. They watched the movie over and over again and cheered when a band of heroes in a galaxy far, far away, used "the force" to battle evil. Watching summer blockbusters became standard practice for millions of teenagers and brought filmmakers huge profits. But by the early 1980s, teens had a whole new universe to explore—the world of computer games.

The best present I ever got was my Walkman [cassette player]. In a small house where I shared a room with my little sister, that thing was an escape, privacy whenever I needed it.

—CHRISTINA MANDELSKI, FOURTEEN, SOUTH FLORIDA, 1984

CHAPTER
EIGHT

TEENAGERS IN THE DIGITAL AGE

By the early 1980s, the U.S. economy had slumped into a deep recession. The price of goods and services rose, and the purchasing power of money shrank. An oil shortage caused long lines at gas stations. Many teenagers found it hard to find part-time jobs. They felt uncertain about the future and worried that they would not have enough money for college. The divorce rate rose, and more teens lived in single parent households. Alcohol and marijuana use by high school students increased. Yet while social problems weighed heavily, a technological revolution took off with lightning speed.

WOW TECHNOLOGY

For decades, computers had been so large and expensive

that only corporations, the government, and other organizations owned them. These huge computers took up entire rooms and needed trained engineers and programmers to run and maintain them. But in the 1970s, engineers discovered how to store most of a computer's functions on a miniature electronic component called a microchip. Microprocessors (computer processing systems contained on microchips) allowed engineers to develop small computers that could be used by individuals. In the early 1980s, engineers continued to refine the technology, until personal computers (PCs) were inexpensive and simple enough for home use. PC sales exploded.

From the beginning, teenagers enthusiastically embraced the new technology. They learned the ins and outs of computers before their parents. According to a 1983 article in *Time* magazine, teenagers take to computers "not as just another obligation imposed by adult society but as a game, a pleasure, a tool, a system that fits naturally into their lives. Unlike anyone over 40, these children have grown up with TV screens; the computer is a screen that responds to them, hooked to a machine that can be programmed to respond the way they want it to. That is power."

Teenagers used early computers for games. Pac-Man and Donkey Kong were popular. Within the space of a few years, teens had hundreds of different games to choose from. They spent hours trying to reach the

Computers offered teens a new activity: electronic games. Electronic gaming technology developed quickly in the 1980s to include gaming systems such as Atari, Sega, and Nintendo.

next game level and beat their best score. Teenagers also bought handheld electronic games. They carried their Game Boys in their pockets and played at school, on the bus, and everywhere in between. Teenage infatuation with computers led to a multimillion-dollar industry.

Apple Computer, a California company, donated thousands of computers to schools, and educators focused on making sure students became computer literate. Teenagers soon used computers for far more than games. They used word processors to write reports. They used reading, math, science, and language programs to sharpen their skills. Some teenagers learned programming languages and wrote their own computer programs.

SEX SELLS

When they weren't playing computer games, many teenagers in the 1980s shopped. Designers displayed logos on the outside of clothing and accessories, and owning the right clothing brands became even more important to teens. Designer jeans were a must for the well-dressed high school student. Each had a trendy label on the pocket or waistband. Many teenage girls also copied the clothing style of the latest bad-girl singer or actress. For boys, high-priced athletic shoes were a must. Many high school boys saved for months to purchase a pair of Air Jordan basketball shoes, named after basketball star Michael Jordan.

Designers sometimes used risqué advertising to lure teenage buyers. In 1981 fifteen-year-old actress Brooke Shields posed in sexy photos to sell Calvin Klein jeans. In one television commercial, Shields wore skintight jeans and purred, "You know what comes between me and my Calvins? Nothing." The ad caused a huge controversy. Stations from New York to California banned it from the airwaves.

Fashion-conscious teenage girls imitated their favorite models and wore tight jeans. They often had to lie down and hold their breath to zip up their pants. As being model thin became the fashion, teenage girls worried about their weight. Some became obsessed with being thin and developed eating disorders. Teens with anorexia nervosa starved themselves. Those with bulimia ate huge meals and then made themselves vomit. Doctors and scientists began to study eating disorders in teenagers. This led to a national campaign to promote healthy eating habits for teens.

Another frightening health concern came to light in the early 1980s. Scientists identified the human immunodeficiency virus (HIV). The virus causes the illness acquired immunedeficiency syndrome (AIDS), which attacks the body's immune system and can be fatal. Many people lived in fear of AIDS. They did not know how the virus was passing from person to person. Many thought that touching an infected person or breathing the same air could spread the disease.

An Indiana teen named Ryan White helped educate the public and dispel the myths surrounding AIDS. White was born with hemophilia, a blood-clotting disorder. As part of his treatment, he received many blood transfusions. When he was thirteen, White contracted AIDS from a transfusion. He wanted to live a normal life, go to school, and hang out with friends in spite of the disease. His school refused to allow White to attend. The school board, parents, teachers, and students feared other students would contract AIDS from casual contact with White.

White and his family fought the ruling, and he eventually returned to school. "I was labeled a trouble maker, my mom an unfit mother, and I was not welcome anywhere," he said. But politicians, entertainers, athletes, and movie stars supported White. He appeared on several television talk shows and on the covers of many magazines. He was also the subject

Ryan White *(left)* fought against ignorance and prejudice about AIDS. He died in 1990 at the age of eighteen.

of a television movie, *The Ryan White Story*. White's media appearances gave the nation accurate information about AIDS. His courage, determination, and positive outlook inspired many people before his death in 1990.

MUST-SEE ENTERTAINMENT

In the 1980s, filmmakers spent millions of dollars making blockbuster movies designed to appeal to teenagers. The films had bigger-than-life special effects, plots full of adventure, and plenty of action. Teens watched *Raiders of the Lost Ark* (1981), *ET: The Extra-Terrestrial* (1982), *Back to the Future* (1985), and *Batman* (1989) two, three, or four times. Teen audiences in the 1980s also liked a good laugh. Comedies such as *Fast Times at Ridgemont High* (1982), *Risky Business* (1983), *The Breakfast Club* (1985), and *Ferris Bueller's Day Off* (1986) became instant classics.

Many adults thought the new crop of films contained too much nudity, bad language, and violence. In 1984 the Motion Picture Association of America added a new film rating, PG-13, to keep children under the age of thirteen from watching inappropriate films.

On television, teenagers and adults watched *Happy Days*, *Family Ties*, *The Cosby Show*, and *Growing Pains*. Their story lines often involved the battle between the generations, played for laughs. *Family Ties*, for example, featured two hippie parents dealing with their

The Cosby Show starring Bill Cosby *(right)* was one of the first television programs to show a stable upper-middle-class African American family, including son Theo, played by Malcolm-Jamal Warner *(left)*. It aired from 1984 until 1992.

more straitlaced children. *The Cosby Show* broke new ground when it showed a stable, upper-middle-class African American family. In the show, two successful parents comically fought to keep their teenage children as interested in school as they were in clothes and dating.

Other shows were geared just toward teenagers. *Square Pegs, Head of the Class*, and *A Different World* had young casts and story lines centered on school, teen social life, and dating. Teenagers and their concerns and interests continued to be a gold mine for the entertainment industry.

ALL KINDS OF ROCK

In 1981 the cable network Music Television (MTV) began showing music videos. Some music videos followed the story of the song's lyrics. Others were concert videos. Still other videos were just a good excuse to showcase dance moves, trendy clothes, and interesting locations. Whatever the format, these short films were an extremely effective marketing tool for musicians. MTV aired music videos twenty-four hours a day, and teenagers became huge fans. Many young people watched MTV for hours each day.

Many recording artists, including Madonna and Michael Jackson, saw their careers take off after releasing music videos with brilliant choreography and lavish sets. But many one-hit wonders also found a home on MTV. "Mickey" by Toni Basil, "Come On Eileen" by Dexy's Midnight Runners, "Take On Me" by A-Ha, and "Relax" by Frankie Goes to Hollywood became enduring classics, even if their singers never had another big U.S. hit. Music videos accommodated rock and roll's many genres— hard rock, soft rock, Latin music, heavy metal, punk, funk, dance, and pop. Each had its own unique sound and its own teenage fans.

Rap music also became popular on MTV in the 1980s. It had its roots in urban streets and clubs. Rappers speak in rhyming verse to a strong beat. They use their raps to tell their life stories or speak out about social problems. Teenagers danced to rap music with a style called break dancing, or street dancing. Break-dancers often competed against one another at parties or on the streets. Hip-hop and gangsta rap evolved into a lifestyle with its own language, dress code, and music.

Whatever type of music teens listened to, personal portable stereos changed how they listened. The Walkman cassette tape player was developed in Japan in 1979 and in the early 1980s was heavily promoted to the U.S. teen market. The device ran on two AA batteries and allowed teenagers to listen to music in private, through lightweight headphones, anywhere they went. In the mid-1980s, the compact disc (CD) became a popular format for all kinds of music. CDs had their own portable player—the Discman.

THE WEB

The Walkman and the Discman paved the way for a host of new technologies that kept teenagers in their own private worlds. In the 1990s, scientists and engineers worked out the technical challenges of electronic mail, or e-mail. The global communications network called the Internet took off in this era. A teen with access to a PC could connect to a huge database called the World Wide Web and instantly find information on any topic imaginable. Teenagers used the Web as a research tool for school reports. They read newspapers and magazines online. They also got up-to-the-minute sports scores and information on fashion trends, movies, and music.

The Internet gave teenagers a new way to communicate with one another. E-mail was easy, convenient, and cheap. It allowed teens to send messages to their friends any time of the day or night. They could also find new friends with similar interests and communicate with them in chat rooms. Although the new technology gave teenagers access to people and information from around the globe, it caused a drop in face-to-face social activities. Many young people began to spend less time hanging out in person and more time hanging out on their computers.

MUSIC AND ENTERTAINMENT IN THE '90S

Computers were an important part of many teenagers' lives in the 1990s, but music, television, and movies were still essential to teen culture. Boy bands Color Me Badd, Backstreet Boys, and NSYNC sold millions of CDs. With perfectly blended voices and intricate choreography, boy bands drove teenage girls wild.

A form of alternative rock called grunge also gained popularity in the 1990s. Kurt Cobain and his band Nirvana brought this musical style into the mainstream. Their biggest hit was "Smells Like Teen Spirit" (1991). Grunge was marked by heavy guitar, strong drums, and lyrics that dealt with pain, anger, frustration, and dark

Kurt Cobain *(right)* and grunge band Nirvana perform in Seattle, Washington, in 1990. Nirvana helped bring alternative music into the mainstream.

humor. The music was an antidote to bubblegum pop music (such as the boy bands) and all that was slick and packaged in American culture.

In 1992 a new genre of television was born: reality TV. The first reality show was MTVs *The Real World*. On the show, seven strangers in their late teens and early twenties live in a house together. Cameras record their daily interactions. The show proved so popular with teenagers that other networks copied the premise. Reality shows became some of the most popular programs on television. Animated comedies for teenagers also hit the airwaves in the 1990s. *Beavis and Butthead* and *South Park* pushed the limits of rude, crude, and stupid humor. Many teenagers loved them.

At the movies, *Clueless* (1995) became a teen classic. In the film, two rich, spoiled girls at Beverly Hills High School in California take a new "clueless" student under their wing for a makeover. The film lampooned teen obsessions with clothes and makeup and relied heavily on teen slang. But it also showed a generally happy, diverse teen crowd of white, African American, gay, rich, and middle-class kids.

In a more serious vein, *Titanic* smashed all box office records in 1997. The movie told the fictional story of two teenage lovers, Jack and Rose, aboard the real-life passenger ship the RMS *Titanic* (which sank in the Atlantic Ocean in 1912). Stunning special effects, lavish sets, a tragic young love story, and heartthrob Leonardo Di Caprio drew teenagers to the film again and again.

Late in the decade, a spate of successful teen comedies hit the theaters. *Can't Hardly Wait* (1998), *10 Things I Hate About You* (1999), and *She's All That* (1999) covered familiar territory—the failures and triumphs of high school life. But with the latest in clothes, slang, and sound track music, they appealed to a new crop of teens.

A DECADE OF FEAR

The 1990s was a decade of fear for many teenagers. The United States faced attacks from foreign and homegrown terrorists. On February 16, 1993, foreign-born radical Muslims with ties to the al-Qaeda terrorist network exploded a truck bomb at the World Trade Center in New York City. The midday bombing killed six people and injured more than one thousand. On April 19, 1995, U.S.-born Timothy McVeigh bombed the Alfred P. Murrah Federal Building, a government office complex, in Oklahoma City, Oklahoma. McVeigh was a U.S. Army veteran with radical antigovernment sympathies. The bombing killed 168 people, including many children, and injured hundreds more. These events, replayed again and again on television, made teenagers feel vulnerable and unsafe.

A series of school shootings also fueled teenagers' fears. The worst case occurred on April 20, 1999. Seventeen-year-old Dylan Klebold and eighteen-year-old Eric Harris went to Columbine High School in Littleton, Colorado, armed with a semiautomatic handgun, rifles, shotguns, and bombs. They opened fire on their classmates, killing twelve students and one teacher and injuring many others before taking their own lives.

As the new millennium approached, some Americans feared that computer technology would bring about a global disaster. Most computers

Students and residents of Littleton, Colorado, and nearby cities hold a vigil on the first anniversary of the Columbine High School shootings. The violent episode in 1999 shocked the community and the nation.

have automatic time and date software. But due to a programming glitch, computers were not prepared to automatically roll over to the year 2000. People feared that this glitch, called the Y2K bug, would cause computer systems to fail. In a world where computers run banking, communications, travel and transport, and power networks, such a failure would result in massive problems.

Computer programmers worked to fix the Y2K bug. But many people still feared that the bug would cause widespread chaos. They worried that banks would run out of money and stores would run out of food and supplies. Some feared that their communities would be left without water and electricity. Looting and other crimes would follow. To prepare for Y2K, concerned families stocked up on canned goods, bottled water, and other supplies. A few people even headed to remote locations, where they believed they would be safe from looters.

However, the new millennium arrived without major incident. Computers had not wrecked society. In fact, the world would become even more connected by and dependent on technology in the decade to come. And teenagers led the way into this new, faster than fast, nanosecond world.

> *Everybody needs to get involved in community service. Everybody. It's not a choice, it's an obligation.*
>
> —MARISSA RIDGLEY, ANCHORAGE, ALASKA, 2010

CHAPTER NINE

TWENTY-FIRST CENTURY TEENAGERS

As the second decade of the twenty-first century begins, nearly thirty million teenagers live in the United States. More than half live in two-income households. Most teens over sixteen work at part-time jobs and have disposable income. Marketing gurus estimate that teenagers are responsible for more than $200 billion in purchases. This economic power makes teenagers a vital link in the nation's economy. Retailers know they must appeal to teens if they want their products to succeed. Manufacturers work to hook young people on their merchandise so they will continue to buy it as adults.

RU CONNECTED?

One sector of the economy that would crumble without teenage dollars is technology. High-tech electronic components have changed the way young people communicate with the world. It has also changed the way teenagers spend their free time.

The vast majority of teens own a cell phone. Many young people get their first cell phone at the age of twelve. In 2009 almost 60 percent of twelve-year-olds owned a cell phone, up from 18 percent in 2004. Among teens ages thirteen to seventeen, 78 percent own a cell phone. For decades, teens have enjoyed chatting with their friends on the phone. Cell phones allow them to chat anywhere, anytime.

But talking isn't the only way teens use cell phones. In the 2000s, text messaging, or texting, became the primary method of teen communication. Between 2007 and 2010, texting increased 566 percent. Texting surpasses face-to-face contact, e-mail, instant messaging, and voice calling among teens.

Texting uses a component of cell phone service to allow users to send brief written messages. Fourteen- to seventeen-year-old girls send an average of one hundred messages a day using a shorthand language of initials, numbers, and abbreviations. Some educators worry that frequent texting disrupts students' ability to spell and use correct grammar. They fear the long-term effect texting might have on the writing ability of American youth.

In the twenty-first century, cell phones are the primary communication tool among teens.

THE INTERNET

Teenagers rely on the Internet, and most of them use it every day. They use it to show the world who they are and what they care about. A 2010 survey showed that more than 80 percent of teens ages fourteen to seventeen access social networking websites. Sites such as Facebook and MySpace help teens connect with friends and relatives. Teen users post comments, photos, videos, artwork, and stories. They connect with friends via instant messages (IMs) and find other teens with similar interests by joining online communities.

Teenagers use the Internet for more than a communications hub. The Web has changed the way they get information. Teens access information on dieting, physical fitness, and health-related topics. They read about current events and politics. Teenagers watch film trailers, music videos, and video clips of their friends, celebrities, and politicians. They also buy books, clothing, and music online and learn about job openings.

Teenagers are learning to be more careful about their Internet use. High-quality academic information is available to help them with their studies. But since cyberspace is uncensored, anyone can post information on a website, regardless of whether it's accurate or unbiased. As Internet usage becomes commonplace, teens are learning to filter out legitimate research sites from those filled with a user's personal bias or prejudice.

The Internet also gives teenagers more flexibility in purchasing music. Instead of having to buy an entire CD to hear a favorite song, the MP3 audio format allow teens to download music files from the Internet and create personalized music lists. Small, portable MP3 players hold thousands of songs. The most popular model is the iPod—considered a must-have item by some teens.

CYBER DANGER

Computers and the Internet have given teenagers the ability to see and communicate with the world. But technology has also brought new dangers. Teenagers face moral decisions with each click. When they write reports for school, they have to choose whether to copy information from the Internet or create original work. Teenagers of every generation have found ways to cheat. For twenty-first century teens, it's simply easier. Modern teens also have distractions beeping at them from all directions, pulling their focus away from their studies. In addition, they have to choose which sites to visit and learn to avoid inappropriate content.

The Internet has brought a new form of bullying into some teenagers' lives—cyberbullying. All too frequently a bully sends harassing e-mails or instant messages to a peer. Bullies can also post negative or insulting remarks about a classmate or spread rumors on the Internet. They send hateful text messages or photos via cell phones. These actions contribute to feelings of depression, loss of self-esteem, and loneliness in the victim. According to a fourteen-year-old girl from Illinois who was bullied, "It [made] me depressed a lot. . . . I would come home and just cry. It really hurt."

Sexting—sending nude or partially nude photos to a phone or Web site—is another social problem unique to twenty-first century teenagers. More than 90 percent of teens take and send photos with their cell phones. So parents find it difficult to stop the practice of sexting. Most of the sexting messages are sent privately to a boyfriend or a girlfriend. However, the photos can easily be forwarded to other phones or posted online.

Sexting can have serious consequences. Some states have attempted to control teen sexting by treating it as a legal issue. State and local authorities have charged teens with the crime of child pornography for sending, forwarding, or selling sexually explicit photos of minors. Possession of child pornography is a serious crime, and teens found guilty of the crime can serve time in detention centers. Some reports show that sexting is also used in cyberbullying and online harassment. And sexting can attract adult sexual predators, who often lurk in chat rooms and social networking sites looking for young victims.

BECOMING BEAUTIFUL

As they have for decades, advertisers sell young people the promise that if they are beautiful, their lives will be wonderful. Teenagers see image after image of the perfect face, hair, and body. They are bombarded with ads for products that guarantee to make them popular and attractive. But some adults worry that this bombardment is doing more harm than ever before. They question whether twenty-four-hour TV, Internet access, and a growing culture of celebrity-worship are pushing teens into unhealthy behaviors.

The flood of advertising and celebrity images informs teens they should have no fat on their bodies and should have a high degree of muscle tone. Teenage boys work out to get "six pack" stomach muscles. Girls strive to be rail thin and fit into size 0 or 2 clothing. The obsession to be thin negatively affects many teenagers. Cases of anorexia nervosa and bulimia are increasing.

It is difficult to get accurate statistics on teenage eating disorders because many young people hide the disorder from their families. However, the National Eating Disorders Association estimates that more than one-half of teenage girls and nearly one-third of teenage boys use unhealthy weight control behaviors such as skipping meals, fasting, smoking cigarettes, vomiting, and taking laxatives. Eating disorders are also found in younger and younger girls, some as young as seven. Plastic surgery has also increased among teenagers. Some teens take extreme measures to correct imagined flaws.

TEEN OFFENDERS

Parents and other teen advocates worry that high school students face more—and more serious—violence. Criminal gangs have grown in size and influence. Many schools have installed metal detectors to keep guns out of schools. Other school districts bring in drug-sniffing dogs to check lockers and cars for illegal substances.

Teen crime is on the rise, and the age of offenders is dropping. Some communities are attempting to deal with this trend by enforcing curfews for teenagers. In Miami, Florida, teenagers seventeen or younger must be off the streets by eleven P.M. on weekdays and by midnight on weekends. Police officers pick up violators and take them home or to a police station. Repeat offenders face possible fines. They may also be ordered to attend family counseling. Most teenagers and many parents are against the measures. "Getting arrested for not being home on time, that's bizarre," said high school senior Kristin Ragland. "That goes against your constitutional rights to . . . freedom."

Another growing trend is teen courts. These courts developed from the idea that an offender's peers would have more of an impact than adults in sentencing a teenager. "I think it's fair, and it's a lot easier to talk about what you did with other kids," said fifteen-year-old Layla Foreman.

Teen courts are generally used for offenders between the ages of ten and fifteen who have no prior arrests. Their crimes are minor, such as shoplifting or disorderly conduct. In teen courts, offenders admit their guilt and agree to accept the sentence given to them by a jury of their peers. The volunteer jury determines the sentence based on a range of sentencing options for each offense. The goal is to hold young offenders accountable for minor illegal behavior while clearing the arrest from their criminal records.

A group of young teens sign a memorial quilt near Ground Zero in New York for those killed on September 11, 2001, during the worst terrorist attack in U.S. history. Al-Qaeda terrorists hijacked four commercial jets filled with passengers. The terrorists flew two planes into the World Trade Center in New York City and a plane into the Pentagon (the headquarters of the U.S. military just outside Washington, D.C.). The fourth plane crashed in a field in rural Pennsylvania.

AN ARMY OF COMPASSION

Although teen crime is on the rise, the number of young people who spend time helping others has also increased. Twenty-first century teenagers volunteer in their communities more often than previous generations of teens. A 2005 survey showed that more than 30 percent of teens ages sixteen to eighteen volunteer for national or community projects. That percentage dropped slightly in the following years, but teens still volunteer at a much higher rate than adults. "I need to do something for the world," explained sixteen-year-old Eduardo Alcocer. "I feel like I want to do something positive. It doesn't have to be big, but some positive contribution."

Some teenagers visit nursing homes and play cards with the residents. Others make lunches at local homeless shelters or deliver food to elderly or ill people who cannot leave their homes. During the summer, teenagers help build or repair homes in low-income neighborhoods. "It's fun, and it's better than watching TV," said Michael Cruz, a tenth grader from New York.

SOCIETY'S TRENDSETTERS

Going to the movies is still the most popular activity for teenagers. Filmmakers have pushed the limits of special effects with computer graphics (CG). CG is particularly effective in fantasy and science-fiction movies, where filmmakers can seamlessly blend live action with fantastical sets and effects. All around the country, teens camped out at movie theaters to be the first to see *The Lord of the Rings* trilogy (2001–2003), the *Pirates of the Caribbean* series (2003–2011), *Cloverfield* (2008), and *The Dark Knight* (2008). In 2009 the fantasy *Avatar* replaced *Titanic* as the top box office hit of all time so far.

But movie ticket sales and DVD rentals suggest that teens still enjoy a good low-tech story too. Adventure, romance, and high school drama continued to appeal. *Save the Last Dance* (2001), *A Knight's Tale* (2001), *Bend It Like Beckham* (2002), *Mean Girls* (2004), and *Juno* (2007) were all teen hits.

Many teenage boys and some girls enjoy multiplayer online role-playing games such as *World of Warcraft* (WoW). Many teens spend hours strategizing with teammates around the world to defeat online opponents. Reading for enjoyment has increased among teenagers. In series such as *Twilight*, readers avidly follow the characters from one book to the next. On TV, *Glee*, a musical comedy about an Ohio high school show chorus, has a huge teenage following. Reality shows such as *American Idol* and *Sixteen and Pregnant* are also popular.

Modern teenagers are concerned with protecting the environment. They are more likely to be blind to racial and cultural differences than adults. Most teenagers do not feel that obtaining wealth is the most important thing in life. In 2007 the Associated Press and MTV asked a group of teenagers, "What makes you happy?" Their answers surprised many adults. The majority of teenagers answered, "spending time with family."

Twilight by Stephenie Meyer became a teen reading phenomenom toward the end of the first decade of the 2000s. The book and its sequels were made into movies starring young actors.

Teenagers are society's trendsetters. Their history was built by the experiences of many diverse groups of young people. Different genders, ethnic groups, social classes, regions, and religions all played a part in what has become known as the American teenager. Teenagers of every generation have examined the world around them and searched for identity. They have tested their strengths and abilities. They have experimented with new clothing styles, listened to all kinds of music, watched movies and TV shows, and thought about the world's problems. It has never been easy, for the teenage years are a time of learning and discovery—for this generation and the next.

Left: Mickey Rooney and Judy Garland pose for a publicity still for *Love Finds Andy Hardy* (1938). In the 1930s and 1940s, screen teens were usually wholesome, fun-loving, well-behaved—and white. Misbehaving was limited to bragging or fudging the truth, and romantic relationships began and ended with innocent kisses.

Below: In the 1950s and 1960s, happy-go-lucky comedies were still a staple of teen movies. But movies sometimes took a darker look at the younger generation. In 1955's *Blackboard Jungle (below)*, Glenn Ford *(left)* plays a teacher in a tough urban boys' school. He reaches out to student Sidney Poitier *(right)*. Poitier later played a teacher in a gritty high school in *To Sir with Love* (1967).

Above: Based on Jane Austen's 1815 novel *Emma*, the hit movie comedy *Clueless* (1995) follows the story of a modern high school girl who solves everyone's problems but her own. *Clueless* featured a fairly diverse cast of characters—wealthy, middle-class, white, African American, high achievers, slackers, gay, and straight.

Below: The TV show *Glee* debuted in 2009. Set in an Ohio high school, its unique format includes comedy, drama, singing, and dancing. Like *Clueless*, *Glee* has a large, diverse cast, including the adult teachers and parents of the teen characters. Merchandising tie-ins, aimed mostly at a young market, include song releases on iTunes, a karaoke game, holiday gift sets, clothing, and accessories.

1880–1920	More than 23 million immigrants come to the United States, mostly from southern and eastern Europe.
1889	Jane Addams and Ellen Gates Starr establish Hull House—a community center—in Chicago, Illinois.
1890	Reports indicate that just 6 percent of fourteen- to seventeen-year-olds attend high school in the United States. Jacob Riis photographs inner-city life and publishes *How the Other Half Lives*.
1899	Illinois passes the Juvenile Court Act and establishes the first juvenile court in the United States.
1904	The National Child Labor Committee mounts an anti-child labor movement.
1914	The Great War (World War I) breaks out in Europe.
1916	The U.S. Congress passes the Keating-Owen Act to set the minimum working age at fourteen for factories and sixteen for mines.
1918	World War I ends.
1920	Prohibition goes into effect, making alcohol illegal in the United States. Station KDKA in Pittsburgh, Pennsylvania, ushers in the age of radio.
1924	Teens Nathan Leopold and Richard Loeb kidnap and murder Bobby Franks.
1929	The stock market crashes, and the Great Depression begins.
1933	More than 25 percent of Americans are out of work. Prohibition ends.
1935	President Franklin D. Roosevelt launches the National Youth Administration (NYA) to keep at-risk teens in school.
1937	Mickey Rooney stars in his first Andy Hardy movie, *A Family Affair*.

1937   Three thousand teens wait outside the Paramount Theater in New York City to see the King of Swing, Benny Goodman.

1938   Cab Calloway publishes his *Hepster's Dictionary for Cool Kats and Jolly Dollies*.

1939   Batman makes his first appearance in a comic book. Sixteen-year-old Judy Garland stars in *The Wizard of Oz*. World War II begins.

1941   The United States enters World War II.

1942   The Great Depression ends.

1944   *Seventeen* magazine begins publication. Teen canteens, or recreation centers, open across the United States.

1945   World War II ends. The Cold War begins.

1946–1964   More than 76 million children are born in the United States during the postwar baby boom.

1952   *Bandstand*, a teen TV dance show, debuts in Philadelphia, Pennsylvania.

1954   School segregation is declared unconstitutional by the U.S. Supreme Court in *Brown v. Board of Education*. RCA introduces the first television to broadcast in color.

1955   Chevrolet markets a "hot car" to teens. The film *Rebel Without a Cause* is released. Movie star James Dean dies in a car accident.

1956   *Rock Around the Clock* is the first hugely successful film marketed to teenagers. Elvis Presley appears on *The Ed Sullivan Show*.

1957   *Bandstand* becomes a national TV program and is renamed *American Bandstand*.

1960   Motown Record Corporation opens in Detroit, Michigan.

1961   John F. Kennedy becomes the youngest elected U.S. president.

1963   Kennedy is assassinated in Dallas, Texas.

1964   President Lyndon B. Johnson signs the Civil Rights Act of 1964, ending racial segregation and outlawing many types of discrimination. The Beatles arrive in the United States.

1965   Johnson signs the National Voting Rights Act, ending voting practices that discriminated against African Americans. The United States sends combat troops to Vietnam.

1967   *In re Gault*, a landmark U.S. Supreme Court case, granted teens accused of a crime the same basic rights as adults.

1968   President Lyndon Johnson signs the Civil Rights Act of 1968 to extend protection against discrimination in housing.

1969   In *Tinker v. Des Moines Independent School System*, the Supreme Court rules that public-school students have basic free-speech rights on school grounds.

1971   Congress passes the Twenty-sixth Amendment to the U.S. Constitution, making eighteen the minimum voting age.

1972   Title IX of the Education Amendments gives girls the same opportunities to play team sports in high school as boys.

1973   The United States ends its military involvement in the Vietnam War. Vice President Spiro Agnew resigns.

1974   President Richard Nixon resigns as a result of the Watergate scandal.

1975   *Jaws* sets the pattern for summer blockbuster movies.

1979   Japanese engineers develop the Walkman, a personal stereo.

1981 Music Television (MTV) begins showing music videos. International Business Machines releases the IBM PC.

1984 Apple Computers releases the Apple Macintosh. The Motion Picture Association of America adds a new film rating, PG-13.

1990s Internet and e-mail use grows dramatically.

1991 Grunge band Nirvana hits the music charts with "Smells Like Teen Spirit."

1992 *The Real World*, TV's first reality show, begins.

1993 Terrorists bomb the World Trade Center in New York, New York.

1995 Timothy McVeigh bombs a government office complex in Oklahoma City, Oklahoma.

1999 Seventeen-year-old Dylan Klebold and eighteen-year-old Eric Harris kill twelve students, one teacher, and themselves at Columbine High School in Littleton, Colorado. The Y2K computer bug becomes a worldwide concern.

2001 Apple releases the first iPod. Terrorists destroy the World Trade Center in New York City and damage the Pentagon in Washington, D.C. Altogether, about three thousand people are killed in the attacks.

2005 More than 30 percent of teens volunteer for national or community projects.

2009 Almost 60 percent of twelve-year-olds and about 78 percent of teens own cell phones.

2010 Miami, Florida, begins enforcing curfews for teenagers. More than 80 percent of teens use social networking sites. *Glee*, a sitcom set in an Ohio high school, wins four Emmy awards.

SOURCE NOTES

6 Elliott West, *Growing Up with the Country: Childhood on the Far Western Frontier* (Albuquerque: University of New Mexico Press, 1989), 73.

7 Ibid.

8 Tamara K. Hareven, *Family Time and Industrial Time* (New York: Cambridge University Press, 1982), 193.

8 Jane Addams, *The Spirit of Youth and the City Streets* (New York: Macmillan, 1912), 107-108.

9 Thomas Hine, *The Rise and Fall of the American Teenager* (New York: HarperCollins, 1999), 126.

11 Lucy Larcom, *A New England Girlhood* (Boston: Houghton, Mifflin, 1892), 166.

11–12 Charles Loring Brace, *The Dangerous Classes of New York, and Twenty Years' Work among Them* (New York: Wynkoop & Hallenbeck, 1872), 13.

12 Ibid., 322.

13 Addams, 16, 161.

14 Randolph S. Bourne, *Youth and Life* (Freeport, NY: Books for Libraries Press, 1913), 19.

14 Irving King, *The High-School Age* (Indianapolis: Bobbs-Merrill, 1914), 108.

15 Sara L. Hart, "Working with the Juvenile Delinquent," in *100 Years at Hull-House,* eds. Mary Lynn McCree Bryan and Allen F. Davis (Bloomington: Indiana University Press, 1969), 146.

15 G. Stanley Hall, *Adolescence* (New York: D. Appleton, 1904), xv.

15 Ibid., 407.

18 Addams, 8.

19 Ibid., 76.

20 Ian Whitcomb, *After the Ball: Pop Music from Rag to Rock* (New York: Simon and Schuster, 1973), 16.

21 *Brooklyn Daily Eagle,* "Oppose 'Ragtime' Tunes," May 14, 1901, 1.

21 *New York Times,* "Philadelphia Bans the Trot," January 5, 1912, 9.

21 Ibid., "Polite Dances Are Shown to Society," March 26, 1912, 13.

21 Ibid.

22 Bruce Bliven, "Flapper Jane," *New Republic*, September 9, 1925, 66.

23 F. Scott Fitzgerald, *The Crack-Up* (New York: Charles Scribner's Sons, 1931), 87.

25 Robert S. Lynd and Helen Merrell Lynd, *Middletown: A Study in American Culture* (New York: Harcourt, Brace & World, 1929), 140.

25 Frederick Lewis Allen, *Only Yesterday: An Informal History of the 1920s* (New York: Harper & Row, 1931), 80.

26 Mary Cross, ed., *A Century of American Icons* (Westport, CT: Greenwood Press, 2002), 53.

27 Lynd and Lynd, 266.

28 *The Jazz Singer,* DVD, directed by Allan Crosland (1927; Burbank, CA: Warner Brothers Pictures, 2007).

28–29 Anne Shaw Faulkner, "Does Jazz Put the Sin in Syncopation?" *Ladies' Home Journal*, August 1921, 16.

29 Allen, 78.

30 Ben B. Lindsey and Wainwright Evans, *The Revolt of Modern Youth* (New York: Boni & Liveright, 1925), 58.

30 Lynd and Lynd, 257.

30 *Parents*, "What Adolescents Want," December 1932, 39.

31 Hal Higdon, *The Crime of the Century: The Leopold and Loeb Case* (New York: G. P. Putnam's Sons, 1975), 167.

32 Robert Cohen, ed., *Dear Mrs. Roosevelt: Letters from Children of the Great Depression* (Chapel Hill: University of North Carolina Press, 2002), 33.

33 Maxine Davis, *The Lost Generation: A Portrait of American Youth Today* (New York: Macmillan, 1936), 34.

34 Errol Lincoln Uys, *Riding the Rails: Teenagers on the Move during the Great Depression* (New York: Routledge, 2003), 256.

34 Ibid., 33.

35 Thomas Minehan, *Boy and Girl Tramps of America* (New York: Farrar and Rinehart, 1934), 168.

35 Grace Palladino, *Teenagers: An American History* (New York: Basic Books, 1996), 44.

39 IMDB.com, "Awards for Mickey Rooney," Internet Movie Database, 2010, http://www.imdb.com/name/nm0001682/awards (January 18, 2010).

39 Ray Barfield, *Listening to Radio, 1920–1950* (Westport, CT: Praeger Publishers, 1996), 20.

39–40 Gerald Nachman, *Raised on Radio* (New York: Pantheon Books, 1998), 4.

40 Frank Norris, "The Killer-Diller: The Life and Four-Four Time of Benny Goodman," *Saturday Evening Post*, May 7, 1938, 22.

40 Frank S. Nugent, "Vendetta or a Clarinetist's Revenge," *New York Times*, January 30, 1938, 5.

42 Ione Quinby Griggs, "They Dance All Over Pop's Heaven," *Saturday Evening Post*, December 9, 1944, 24–25.

43 Studs Terkel, *The Good War: An Oral History of World War II* (New York: Pantheon Books, 1984), 38.

43 Ibid., 174.

44 Dorothy Gordon, "As the Youngsters See Juvenile Delinquency," *New York Times Magazine*, August 6, 1944, SM32.

47 Helen Valentine, "Seventeen Says Hello," *Seventeen*, September 1944, 33.

48 Jon Savage, *Teenage: The Creation of Youth Culture* (New York: Viking, 2007), 324.

49 Kitty Kelley, *His Way: The Unauthorized Biography of Frank Sinatra* (New York: Bantam Books, 1986), 74.

50 *Look*, "Are These Our Children?" September 21, 1943, 21.

50 Michael Barson and Steven Heller, *Teenage Confidential* (San Francisco: Chronicle Books, 1998), 41.

50–51 Richard M. Ugland, "The Adolescent Experience during World War II: Indianapolis as a Case Study" (Ph.D. diss., Indiana University, 1977), 260–261.

52 Richard Clendenen and Herbert W. Beaser, "The Shame of America," *Saturday Evening Post*, January 8, 1955, 78.

55 Richard Gehman, "The Nine Billion Dollars in Hot Little Hands," *Cosmopolitan*, November 1957, 72.

55 Dwight MacDonald, "A Caste, a Culture, a Market," *New Yorker*, November 22, 1958, 70.

56 "Brown v. Board of Education," *The National Center for Public Policy Research*, n.d., http://www.nationalcenter.org/brown.html (March 15, 2010).

58 Ellen Levine, ed., *Freedom's Children: Young Civil Rights Activists Tell Their Own Stories* (New York: Avon Books, 1993), 62.

58 Marguerite W. Cullman, "Double Feature—Movies and Moonlight," *New York Times Magazine*, October 1, 1950, 68.

58 Ibid., 69.

59 Olga Druce, "Text of NAB Code," *Variety*, September 17, 1947, 28.

61 *James Dean: Forever Young*, DVD, directed by Michael J. Sheridan (Burbank, CA Warner Brothers Entertainment, 2005).

61 *Rock Around the Clock*, DVD, directed by Fred F. Sears (1956; Culver City, CA: Columbia Pictures Corporation, 2007).

62 Herm Schoenfeld, "Teenagers Like 'Hot Rod' Tempo," *Variety*, January 19, 1955, 54.

64 Joyce Maynard, "An 18-Year Old Looks Back On Life," *New York Times Magazine*, April 23, 1972, SM 11.

65 Terkel, 581.

65 John T. Wolley and Gerhard Peters, "John F. Kennedy: Inaugural Address," American Presidency Project, 2010, http://www.presidency.ucsb.edu/ws/?pid=8032 (March 10, 2010).

65 Annie Gottlieb, *Do You Believe in Magic? The Second Coming of the Sixties Generation* (New York: Times Books, 1987), 34.

65 Landon Y. Jones, *Great Expectations: America and the Baby Boom Generation* (New York: Coward, McCann & Geoghegan, 1980), 65–66.

67 Philip Norman, *Shout! The Beatles in Their Generation* (New York: Fireside, 2005), 191.

72 Dorothy Waleski, "Regulating Student Dress," *NEA Journal: The Journal of the National Education Association*, April 1966, 12.

73 Ralph W. Larkin, *Suburban Youth in Cultural Crisis* (New York: Oxford University Press, 1979), 90.

73–74   Jones, 134.

76   Christina Mandelski, interview with the author, May 11, 2010.

77   Otto Friedrich, "The Computer Moves In," *Time*, January 3, 1983, 23.

78   Shirley Clurman, "Calvin Klein," *People*, January 18, 1982, 97.

79   Ryan White, "Testimony of Ryan White Before the National Commission on AIDS," March 3, 1988, http://www.ryanwhite.com (June 16, 2010).

86   Lauren Heyano, "Teens Serving Now," *Alaska Business Monthly*, May 2010, 27.

89   Sameer Hinduja and Justin W. Patchin, "Cyberbullying Research Summary: Emotional and Psychological Consequences," Cyberbullying Research Center, 2009, http://www.cyberbullying.us/cyberbullying_emotional_consequences.pdf (April 8, 2010).

91   DeNeen L. Brown and Stephen Buckley, "Teens Set to Fight for Right to Party," *Washington Post*, March 4, 1993, B1.

91   Rosemary Zibart, "When Teens Judge One Another," *USA Weekend*, October 18–20, 1996.

92   Sydney Lewis, *A Totally Alien Life-Form* (New York: New Press, 1996), 80.

92   Caroline Kennedy, "Teens Team Up to Give Back," *Time*, March 26, 2007, 57.

93   Ralph Waldo Emerson, "Surprising News about What Makes Teens Happy," *Curriculum Review*, October 2007, 12.

SELECTED BIBLIOGRAPHY

Castleman, Harry, and Walter J. Podrazik. *Watching TV: Six Decades of American Television.* Syracuse, NY: Syracuse University Press, 2003.

Chinn, Sarah E. *Inventing Modern Adolescence: The Children of Immigrants in Turn-of-the-Century America.* New Brunswick, NJ: Rutgers University Press, 2009.

Clement, Elizabeth Alice. *Love for Sale: Courting, Treating, and Prostitution in New York City, 1900–1945.* Chapel Hill: University of North Carolina Press, 2006.

Cross, Mary, ed. *A Century of American Icons.* Westport, CT: Greenwood Press, 2002.

Egendorf, Laura K. *Prosperity, Depression, and War: 1920–1945.* Farmington Hills, MI: Greenhaven Press, 2003.

Lenhart, Amanda. *Social Media and Young Adults.* Washington, DC: Pew Internet & American Life Project, 2010.

Lytle, Mark Hamilton. *America's Uncivil Wars: The Sixties Era from Elvis to the Fall of Richard Nixon.* New York: Oxford University Press, 2006.

Savage, Jon. *Teenage: The Creation of Youth Culture.* New York: Viking, 2007.

Schrum, Kelly. *Some Wore Bobby Sox: The Emergence of Teenage Girls' Culture, 1920–1945.* New York: Palgrave Macmillan, 2004.

Taffel, Ron T. *The Second Family: How Adolescent Power Is Challenging the American Family.* New York: St. Martin's Press, 2001.

Uys, Errol Lincoln. *Riding the Rails: Teenagers on the Move during the Great Depression.* New York: Routledge, 2003.

White, H. Loring. *Ragging It: Getting Ragtime into History (and Some History into Ragtime).* New York: iUniverse, 2005.

BOOKS

Decades of Twentieth-Century America series. Minneapolis: Twenty-First Century Books, 2010.

Gallo, Donald R., ed. *Time Capsule: Short Stories about Teenagers throughout the Twentieth Century*. New York: Dell Laurel-Leaf Books, 1999.

Images and Issues of Women in the Twentieth Century series. Minneapolis: Twenty-First Century Books, 2007.

Josephson, Judith Pinkerton. *Growing Up in a New Century 1890 to 1914*. Minneapolis: Lerner Publications Company, 2003.

Mierau, Christina. *Accept No Substitutes: The History of American Advertising*. Minneapolis: Twenty-First Century Books, 2000.

Sonenklar, Carol. *Anorexia and Bulimia*. Minneapolis: Twenty-First Century Books, 2011.

WEBSITES

American Cultural History: The Twentieth Century
http://kclibrary.lonestar.edu/decades.html
This website presents a series of guides on the art, music, social history, and important events of each decade of the twentieth century.

Merchants of Cool
http://www.pbs.org/wgbh/pages/frontline/shows/cool/index.html
This PBS website reports on the creators and marketers of popular culture for teenagers.

Museum of Broadcast Communications
http://www.museum.tv/
Watch interviews and read original essays on American broadcast media history, browse the Archive of American Television and the Encyclopedia of Television, and watch clips from classic TV shows and commercials.

MOVIES AND TV

Freaks and Geeks: The Complete Series. DVD. Los Angeles: Shout Factory Theater, 2004.
This 1999 TV comedy is set in a Michigan high school in 1980. Junior Lindsay (Linda
Cardellini) decides to jump off the overachiever track and find out what life is like among
the school slackers. Meanwhile, her brother, Sam (John Francis Daley), makes his way through
his freshman year with the help of his nerdy best friends. James Franco, Seth Rogen, and
Jason Segel costar.

Love Finds Andy Hardy. DVD. Burbank, CA: Warner Home Video, 2005.
Fourth in a series of fifteen films made between 1937 and 1946, this hugely popular 1938
movie follows the teenage adventures of Andy Hardy (played by Mickey Rooney) and the
girl next door (Judy Garland).

Real Women Have Curves. DVD. Santa Monica, CA: HBO Home Video, 2003.
This comedy-drama shows a teen dealing with family pressures, cultural traditions, and a
healthy body image. Ana Garcia (America Ferrara) is a slightly overweight Mexican American
teen. Ana's mother wants her to work in the family dressmaking business, but Ana has her
sights set on college.

Rebel Without a Cause. DVD. Burbank, CA: Warner Home Video, 2005.
This 1955 classic juvenile delinquent film stars James Dean as a troubled and lonely high
school student. Natalie Wood and Sal Mineo play the equally lonely kids he befriends.

Smoke Signals. DVD. New York: Miramax Films, 1999.
This comedy about friendship and family was written and directed by and stars Native
Americans. Victor (Adam Beach) and Thomas Builds-the-Fire (Evan Adams) take a road trip
from Idaho to Arizona after the death of Victor's estranged father.

Swing: The Velocity of Celebration. DVD. Arlington, VA: PBS Home Video, 2000.
Episode 6 of the Ken Burns documentary series *Jazz* looks at the music of swing masters Duke
Ellington, Louis Armstrong, Benny Goodman, and many others.